Major Muslim Nations

SOMALIA

ERITREA

Red
Sea

YEMEN

Gulf of Aden

DJIBOUTI

Berbera

Burao

Hargeysa

SOMALIA

ETHIOPIA

Gaalkacyo

INDIAN

OCEAN

Beledweyne

N
W   E
S

Baydhabo

Jawhar

Shabeelle River

Mogadishu

Jubba River

Marka

KENYA

Jamaame

Kismaayo

0   100   200 Miles

0   100   200 Kilometers
Albers Conic Equal-Area Projection

12N

8N

4N

0

40E   44E   48E   52E

Major Muslim Nations

SOMALIA

LEEANNE GELLETLY

MASON CREST PUBLISHERS
PHILADELPHIA

Mason Crest Publishers
370 Reed Road
Broomall, PA 19008
www.masoncrest.com

Copyright © 2010 by Mason Crest Publishers. All rights reserved.
Printed and bound in the Hashemite Kingdom of Jordan.

First printing

1 3 5 7 9 8 6 4 2

Library of Congress Cataloging-in-Publication Data

Gelletly, LeeAnne.
  Somalia / LeeAnne Gelletly.
      p. cm. — (Major Muslim Nations)
  Includes index.
  ISBN 978-1-4222-1395-7 (hardcover) — ISBN 978-1-4222-1425-1 (pbk.)
  1. Somalia—Juvenile literature. I. Title.
  DT401.5.G45 2008
  967.73—dc22
                                    2008042525

Original ISBN: 1-59084-520-X (hc)

TABLE OF CONTENTS

Major Muslim Nations

Dr. Harvey Sicherman, president and director of the Foreign Policy Research Institute, is the author of such books as *America the Vulnerable: Our Military Problems and How to Fix Them* (2002) and *Palestinian Autonomy, Self-Government and Peace* (1993).

Introduction

by Dr. Harvey Sicherman

America's triumph in the Cold War promised a new burst of peace and prosperity. Indeed, the decade between the demise of the Soviet Union and the destruction of September 11, 2001, seems in retrospect deceptively attractive. Today, of course, we are more fully aware—to our sorrow—of the dangers and troubles no longer just below the surface.

The Muslim identities of most of the terrorists at war with the United States have also provoked great interest in Islam and the role of religion in politics. A truly global religion, Islam's tenets are held by hundreds of millions of people from every ethnic group, scattered across the globe. It is crucial for Americans not to assume that Osama bin Laden's ideas are identical to those of most Muslims, or, for that matter, that most Muslims are Arabs. Also, it is important for Americans to understand the "hot spots" in the Muslim world because many will make an impact on the United States.

A glance at the map establishes the extraordinary coverage of our authors. Every climate and terrain may be found and every form of human society, from the nomads of the Central Asian steppes and Arabian deserts to highly sophisticated cities such as Cairo and Singapore. Economies range from barter systems to stock exchanges, from oil-rich countries to the thriving semi-market powers, such as India, now on the march. Others have built wealth on service and shipping.

The Middle East and Central Asia are heavily armed and turbulent. Pakistan is a nuclear power, Iran threatens to become one, and Israel is assumed to possess a small arsenal. But in other places, such as Afghanistan and the Sudan, the horse and mule remain potent instruments of war. All have a rich history of conflict, domestic and international, old and new.

Governments include dictatorships, democracies, and hybrids without a name; centralized and decentralized administrations; and older patterns of tribal and clan associations. The region is a veritable encyclopedia of political expression.

Although such variety defies easy generalities, it is still possible to make several observations.

First, the regional geopolitics reflect the impact of empires and the struggles of post-imperial independence. While centuries-old history is often invoked, the truth is that the modern Middle East political system dates only from the 1920s, when the Ottoman Empire dissolved in the wake of its defeat by Britain and France in World War I. States such as Algeria, Iraq, Israel, Jordan, Kuwait, Saudi Arabia, Syria, Turkey, and the United Arab Emirates did not exist before 1914—they became independent between 1920 and 1971. Others, such as Egypt and Iran, were dominated by foreign powers until well after World War II. Few of the leaders of these states were happy with the territories they were assigned or the borders, which were often drawn by Europeans. Yet the system has endured despite many efforts to change it.

A similar story may be told in South Asia. The British Raj dissolved into India and Pakistan in 1947. Still further east, Malaysia shares a British experience but Indonesia, a Dutch invention, has its own European heritage. These imperial histories weigh heavily upon the politics of the region.

The second observation concerns economics, demography, and natural resources. These countries offer dramatic geographical contrasts: vast parched deserts and high mountains, some with year-round snow; stone-hard volcanic rifts and lush semi-tropical valleys; extremely dry and extremely wet conditions, sometimes separated by only a few miles; large permanent rivers and wadis, riverbeds dry as a bone until winter rains send torrents of flood from the mountains to the sea.

Although famous historically for its exports of grains, fabrics, and spices, most recently the Muslim regions are known more for a single commodity: oil. Petroleum is unevenly distributed; while it is largely concentrated in the Persian Gulf and Arabian Peninsula, large oil fields can be found in Algeria, Libya, and further east in Indonesia. Natural gas is also abundant in the Gulf, and there are new, potentially lucrative offshore gas fields in the Eastern Mediterranean.

This uneven distribution of wealth has been compounded by demographics. Birth rates are very high, but the countries with the most oil are often lightly populated. Over the last decade, a youth "bulge" has emerged and this, combined with increased urbanization, has strained water supplies, air quality, public sanitation, and health services throughout the Muslim world. How will these young people be educated? Where will they work? A large outward migration, especially to Europe, indicates the lack of opportunity at home.

In the face of these challenges, the traditional state-dominated economic strategies have given way partly to experiments with "privatization" and foreign investment. But economic progress has come slowly, if at all, and most people have yet to benefit from "globalization," although there are pockets of prosperity, high technology (notably in Israel), and valuable natural resources (oil, gas, and minerals). Rising expectations have yet to be met.

A third important observation is the role of religion in the Middle East. Americans, who take separation of church and state for granted, should know that most countries in the region either proclaim their countries to be Muslim or allow a very large role for that religion in public life. (Islamic law, Sharia, permits people to practice Judaism and Christianity in Muslim states but only as *dhimmi*, "protected" but second-class citizens.) Among those with predominantly Muslim populations, Turkey alone describes itself as secular and prohibits avowedly religious parties in the political system. Lebanon was a Christian-dominated state, and Israel continues to be a Jewish state. Even where politics are secular, religion plays an enormous role in culture, daily life, and legislation.

Islam has deeply affected every state and people in these regions. But Islamic practices and groups vary from the well-known Sunni and Shiite groups to energetic Salafi (Wahhabi) and Sufi movements. Over the last 20 years especially, South and Central Asia have become battlegrounds for competing Shiite (Iranian) and Wahhabi (Saudi) doctrines, well financed from abroad and aggressively antagonistic toward non-Muslims and each other. Resistance to the Soviet war in Afghanistan brought these groups battle-tested warriors and organizers responsive to the doctrines made popular by Osama bin Laden and others. This newly significant struggle within Islam, superimposed on an older Muslim history, will shape political and economic destinies throughout the region and beyond.

We hope that these books will enlighten both teacher and student about the critical "hot spots" of the Muslim world. These countries would be important in their own right to Americans; arguably, after 9/11, they became vital to our national security. And the enduring impact of Islam is a crucial factor we must understand. We at the Foreign Policy Research Institute hope these books will illuminate both the facts and the prospects.

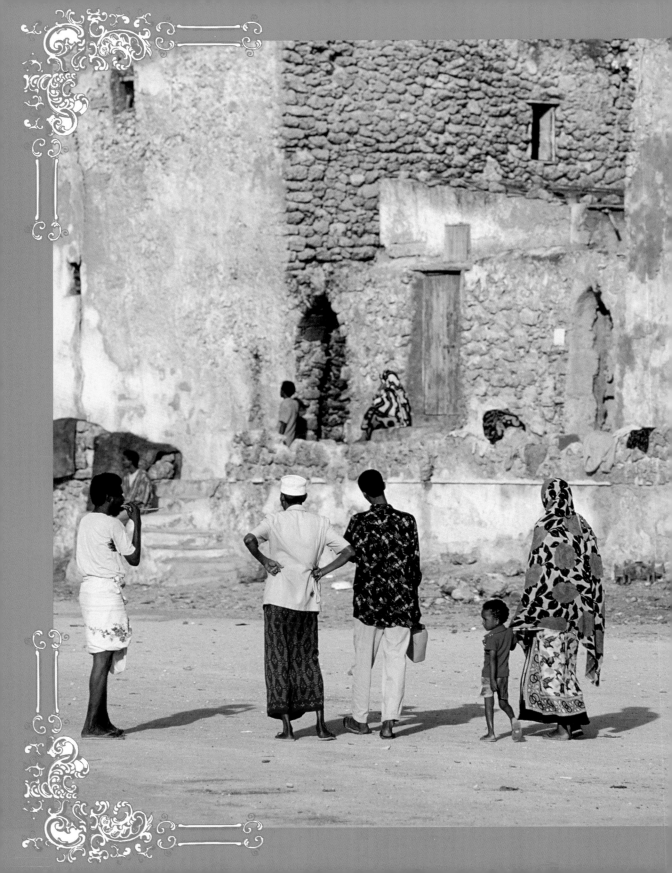

Somalia, an impoverished and war-ravaged country on the Horn of Africa, is home to more than 9 million people. Pictured here is a scene from Mogadishu, the nation's capital.

Place in the World

Located on the northeastern coast of Africa, the desert country of Somalia is home to more than 9 million people who share a common language and religion. Almost all speak Somali and live according to the Islamic faith. More than half are **pastoral nomads**—members of tribes that move from place to place to find food and water for their herds, a difficult task in the dry Somalian climate. The rest have settled in farming regions or live in cities and towns.

The Somalis are a hardy people, known for their ability to carry on in the face of great adversity. They have endured despite centuries of living in a harsh environment plagued by drought, floods, famine, and war.

IMPORTANCE OF CLANS

Somalis have both survived and suffered because of the **clan** system that permeates their society. Most of the people of Somalia belong to a clan, which is a family group whose members can trace their **lineage** to a common ancestor—the clan's founder. The clan network has provided a social framework in which even the very poor can make a living. However, fierce rivalries between clan groups have also affected the country's politics, causing years of violence and hardship for the Somali people.

There are six main clan families in Somalia. All are believed to be descended from two brothers—Samaal and Saab, who belonged to the Quraysh tribe of the prophet Muhammad, the founder of Islam. The four clans claiming direct descent from Samaal—the Daarood, Dir, Isaaq, and Hawiye—make up about 75 percent of the Somali population. Most of the Samaal live as pastoral nomads in the northern part of the country. The two remaining clans—the Digil and the Rahanwayn—claim kinship with Saab. They make up about 20 percent of the Somali population and reside mostly in the south, where they farm the land and raise cattle.

Within each of the six major clans is a complicated structure of subclans. In some cases a single subclan can make up the majority population of a territory, but for the most part, subclans tend to mix together in a given area. The importance of a clan or subclan depends on its size and wealth, usually determined by the number of camels, cattle, sheep, and goats that it owns. Membership in a clan is determined by paternal lineage: the male descendants who can be traced from the clan and subclan's founders, whose names are the same as that of the subclan.

To Somalis, family is identity. Children learn about their clan and even memorize the names of ancestors. Many Somali men have memorized the names of all their male ancestors back to their clan's founder—25 or more generations. Historian Charles Geshekter clearly describes the importance of family background: "When Somalis meet each other, they don't ask, 'Where are you from? Rather, they ask, 'Whom are you from?' Genealogy is to

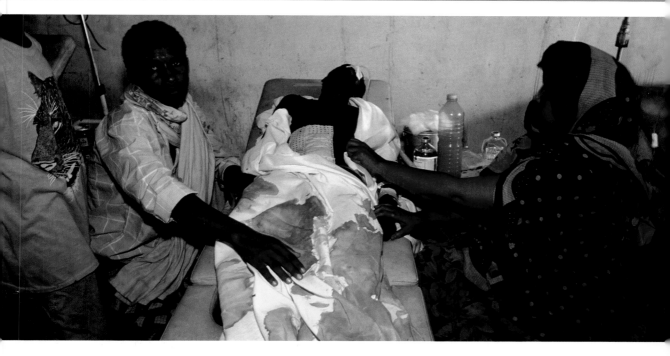

A victim of the seemingly endless clan warfare that has plagued Somalia receives treatment at a hospital.

Somalis what an address is to Americans."

In central and northern Somalia, as pastoral nomads migrated over one another's territory, they often feuded over water resources or land for grazing livestock. In the settled-farming areas of the south, the Digil and Rahanwayn clans fought over trade and religious matters; they also battled the northern nomads who ventured into their territory. Traditionally, such disputes would be judged by elders. Clans have ceremonial heads known as *soldaans* (or sultans), but councils known as *shirs*, composed of all the clan's adult males, handle their internal affairs. Among the Samaal, council elders resolved disagreements, while Saab clans turned to leaders known as *gobweyns* to settle arguments and conflicting claims.

Within the tightly knit clan network, an offense against an individual is an offense against the entire clan or subclan. When an injustice has been committed, the whole clan will quickly respond, sometimes exacting deadly revenge. A Somali who murders a member of another clan brings his guilt for the crime upon all his clan members. Such disputes may be resolved by a clan elder, who designates a fine that the offending clan must pay. But often the clansmen of the dead man will seek revenge on anyone in the killer's clan, regardless of his involvement in the murder.

Although the bonds of the patriarchal clan are strong, a Somali's first loyalty is always to the immediate family—that is, to his brothers. Second to that is allegiance to one's immediate lineage (father), then to the subclan lineage (uncles and grandfather), and finally to the clan family. But first and foremost comes family, as illustrated by the Somali saying: "I and my clan against the world. I and my brother against my clan."

YEARS WITHOUT A GOVERNMENT

Somalia was once known as the Somali Republic, an independent nation created in 1960 when Italian Somaliland and British Somaliland merged. The tumultuous years that followed independence led to a military coup within a decade. The army's leader, General Mohamed Siad Barre, seized power and ruled as dictator for the next 21 years. His government gave way in 1991 to regional control by assorted military strongmen, or warlords. These men used private armies to assume leadership positions within their own clan and to fight for control of various territories in Somalia. To supply and pay their militia fighters in the ongoing conflicts, warlords commonly resorted to looting, kidnapping, and murder.

In the midst of this warfare, northwestern Somalia, home to the Isaaq clan, announced it would secede, or withdraw, from the nation. The breakaway Republic of Somaliland claimed the city of Hargeysa as its capital and set about establishing its own government. A few years later the Harti subclan of the Daarood clan family created a similar nation in the northeast, called Puntland. Both breakaway nations established fairly stable governments and self-sufficient economies. However, as of 2009 neither was recognized as an independent country by the rest of the world.

Meanwhile, most areas of Somalia, including the capital city of Mogadishu, remained wracked by anarchy and civil unrest. Since 1991, at least 14 interim governing bodies have attempted to restore order. The outside world refers to Somalia as a failed state because it has no effective central government.

A LAND OF FREE ENTERPRISE

The absence of government oversight and regulation, however, has allowed some Somalian companies to thrive. Despite its extreme poverty and political, social, and civil troubles, Somalia is home to the most sophisticated telecommunications network in Africa, providing service rated as the best and cheapest on the continent. The largest company in Mogadishu is Telecom Somalia, which employs some 750 people and offers the same mobile phone features available in industrialized nations. In 2001 Telecom Somalia joined with two other cellular-phone companies to create Mogadishu's first local Internet service provider.

Much of the money supporting Somalia's businesses comes from Somalis who have left the country to live and work abroad. These immigrants send portions of their paychecks to relatives back home. Often this money is also invested in the cities or regions these workers came from, supporting local start-up companies, existing businesses, and schools.

Informal codes of honor that have existed for centuries in the clan traditions of Somalia have facilitated business deals and transfers of money. By providing a financial system based on trust, Somalia's tightly knit clan network, while a major source of the country's recent troubles, is also helping to nurture its future economic growth.

Men and boys sit on the steps of a monument in Baidoa. An inland city located between the Jubba and Shabeelle Rivers in southern Somalia, Baidoa is the capital of the country's Bay region.

The Land

Wrapped around the northeast tip of Africa is the comma-shaped land known as Somalia. Its 1,880-mile (3,025-kilometer) coastline, with few natural harbors, runs along the Gulf of Aden to the north and the Indian Ocean to the east. Somalia forms the outer edge of the region known as the Horn of Africa, which also includes the countries of Djibouti, Eritrea, Ethiopia, Kenya, and Sudan. Somalia shares borders with three of these countries: Djibouti to the northwest, and Ethiopia and Kenya to the west.

Slightly smaller than the state of Texas, Somalia covers 246,201 square miles (637,657 sq km). The country is basically low and flat, consisting mostly of dry deserts, savannahs (grassland plains with scattered trees), and **plateaus**. Only to the north, along the Gulf of Aden coast, does the altitude climb into a stretch of low, rugged mountain ranges.

NORTHERN SOMALIA

In Somalia, water is a precious commodity, especially in the northern and central regions of the country. To the far north, along the Gulf of Aden, lies a narrow coastal plain referred to as the Guban, which means "burned from lack of water." Shallow, dry streambeds cover this semidesert region most of the time. However, during rainy seasons, ponds and streams form, and the sparse vegetation turns green. At this time, when the land can support them, nomads bring their herds of cattle, sheep, and goats into the region.

South of the Guban, the land suddenly rises up, forming the steep cliffs of a mountain range that extends from the northwestern border with Ethiopia eastward toward the tip of the Horn of Africa. These mountains average about 3,000 to 7,000 feet (900 to 2,100 meters) above sea level. The tallest peak reaches 7,927 feet

Northern Somalia contains steep cliffs and low, rugged mountains that run eastward from the border with Ethiopia.

Plateaus and low-lying plains make up most of Somalia, the easternmost country on the continent of Africa.

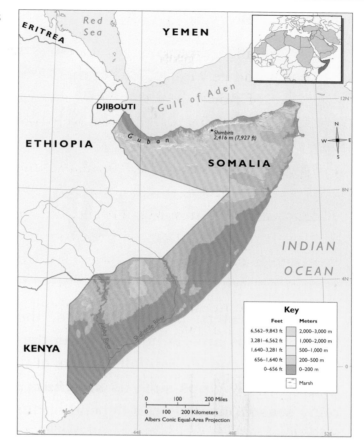

(2,416 meters). Located near the town of Erigavo, it is called Shimbiris (also referred to as Shimber Berris).

From the mountains, the land descends to low valleys and elevated plateaus that feature a few isolated mountain ranges. The Somalis call this extremely arid region, which usually contains dry streambeds, the Ogo. The plateau in the eastern part of the Ogo slopes east toward the Indian Ocean and southeast toward the Nugaal Valley, eventually reaching the Mudug Plain of central Somalia, where it averages less than 600 feet (180 meters) above sea level. Mostly populated by pastoral nomads, this eastern region receives erratic rainfall. During times of severe drought, the area becomes too dry to support any life.

A Somali farmer from the relatively fertile Bay region hauls his sorghum crop to market. Less than 13 percent of Somalia's land is suitable for agriculture—and only about 2 percent is actually cultivated.

In the western part of the Ogo, the plateau extends toward Ethiopia. This area is not as dry as the Ogo's eastern plateau. In fact, there is enough rainfall in parts of these highlands for farmers to grow hardy crops such as **sorghum** and corn. And during the rainy season, nomads can depend on finding filled water holes for their livestock in the region's plains and shallow valleys.

South of the western plateau, extending about 37 miles (60 km) into Ethiopia, lies a broad plain called the **Haud**. This region becomes lush pastureland during the rainy seasons, when grasses and flowers blanket the area and depressions in the land turn into temporary lakes and ponds. Ideal for grazing livestock, the Haud is part of the Ogaden, a region that extends northwest into Ethiopia's southern highlands. Many Somali nomads live in the Ogaden, and its ownership by Ethiopia has often been contested by Somalia.

SOUTHERN SOMALIA

Water is not as scarce in the southern part of Somalia, which contains two permanent rivers—the Shabeelle and the Jubba. Both originate in the west, in the mountains of Ethiopia. The Shabeelle

River, which is 1,243 miles (2,000 km) long, runs southeast through the plateau of central Somalia, before turning sharply about 20 miles (32 km) north of Mogadishu. The Shabeelle then runs parallel to the coastline, eventually meandering into marshland before reaching the Jubba River, located to the west. Only during times of significant rainfall does the Shabeelle flow all the way into the Jubba, which runs about 545 miles (875 km) south from its origin in Ethiopia before entering the Indian Ocean just north of the port city of Kismaayo.

Although most of Somalia is too arid for intensive farming, the

The Geography of Somalia

Location: eastern Africa, with Gulf of Aden to the north and Indian Ocean to the east

Area: (slightly smaller than Texas)
total: 246,201 square miles (637,657 sq km)
land: 242,216 square miles (627,337 sq km)
water: 3,985 square miles (10,320 sq km)

Borders: Djibouti, 36 miles (58 km); Ethiopia, 994 miles (1,600 km); Kenya, 424 miles (682 km)

Climate: mostly tropical and subtropical, with moderate temperatures principally along coastline and at higher altitudes; four seasons: *gu* rains (April to June), *hagaa* dry season (July to September), *dayr* rains (October to November) and *jiilaal* dry season (December to March)

Terrain: narrow northern coastal plain; low mountains in north; central and southern dry savannah plains and plateaus

Elevation extremes:
lowest point: Indian Ocean—0 feet
highest point: Shimbiris—7,927 feet (2,416 meters)

Natural hazards: periodic droughts, summer dust storms over eastern plains; floods during rainy season

Source: Adapted from CIA World Factbook, 2009.

Shabeelle and Jubba enclose a fertile area in which most of Somalia's settled agriculture takes place. Farmers grow corn and cereal grains such as millet and sorghum along both rivers, and they use the ready water supply to irrigate nearby plantations of bananas and citrus fruits. Because there is usually enough moisture to sustain agriculture, most of the country's settled farming population lives in this region. The only other arable land (land that is suitable for farming) is found along coastal regions and in the north, near Hargeysa.

Much of the rest of the southern interior consists of a low plateau that averages about 590 feet (180 meters) above sea level. It is made up of a wide plain, with widespread sand dunes.

CLIMATE

Somalia's climate ranges from tropical to subtropical and from arid to semiarid. Except for the rugged mountains and sandy coastline, daily maximum temperatures in Somalia vary from 85 degrees Fahrenheit (30 degrees Celsius) to 105°F (40°C). Daily low temperatures range from 60°F to 85°F (15°C to 30°C). Temperatures are generally cooler along the coast and at higher mountain altitudes.

Twice a year Somalis find relief from their country's dry weather and hot, dusty winds. The welcome seasonal changes are caused by the **monsoon** winds, which blow from the southwest between April and October. Then the winds change direction, blowing from the northeast until the following April.

The first dry season, known as the **jiilal**, occurs from January to late March. Temperatures are hottest in the south, where nomads living inland are forced to move out of the region as water holes dry up and vegetation dies. In the north, temperatures remain comfortable during this time.

The first major rainfall, referred to as the **gu** rains, usually arrives in April and lasts until June. During this season, Somalia's dry plateaus are transformed into seas of grass and colorful desert flowers, providing abundant pastureland for livestock.

The end of rainfall around July signals the beginning of **hagaa**, a second dry spell. For the next three months, plants and vegetation wither and die from the lack of moisture. People living in the northern regions of Somalia find this season to be the hottest time of year, while those in the southern areas benefit from cooler southwest winds blowing off the Indian Ocean.

A second wet season, called the **dayr** rains, occurs from October to November. The period does not bring as much rainfall as the *gu* rains, usually accounting for about 30 percent of the country's total rainfall. However, it brings enough moisture to once again blanket the plateaus with vegetation.

Average annual rainfall in Somalia is about 11 inches (28 centimeters). Much of northern and northeastern Somalia receives just 2 to 6 inches (5 to 15 cm) per year, while southern Somalia receives an average of 13 to 20 inches (33 to 50 cm).

Somalia periodically endures droughts, but on occasion severe floods strike in lower regions. For example, heavy flooding in southern Somalia in late 1997 killed hundreds and ruined the region's crops. During prolonged droughts, when the country has received little or no rain for several years, rural Somalis in particular suffer from widespread famine. One of Somalia's worst droughts occurred between 1974 and 1975. From 1999 to 2002 a significant lack of rainfall caused a decline in the numbers of livestock and subsequent hunger for many Somalis.

LOSS OF VEGETATION AND WILDLIFE

In 1991 the United Nations (U.N.) estimated that about 14 percent of Somalia contained vegetation. Typical plant life found in the drier areas of the north included trees such as acacia, thorn, baobab, and *Boswellia* and *Commiphora* (sources, respectively, of the gum resins frankincense and myrrh). Other plants included the aloe, *Candelabra euphorbia* (a type of cactus), low bushes, and clumps of grasses. Central and southern areas of Somalia contained many more acacias, as well as eucalyptus, euphorbia, and mahogany trees. Kapok, mango, papaya, and mangrove forests lined the rivers, and many more mangrove trees grew along the coast, especially the area near Mogadishu and from Kismaayo to the Kenyan border.

However, as of 2002, environmental experts estimated that only about 4 percent of Somalia's vegetation remained. Large swaths of forestland, particularly in the southern and central regions of Somalia, had been cut and burned to create charcoal, a common cooking fuel used by Somalis. Besides being sold for domestic use, the charcoal is also shipped to Persian Gulf countries such as Saudi Arabia, Yemen, and the United Arab Emirates.

Up until 1996, Somalia's forests had been protected—first by the government until it collapsed in 1991, and then by warlord Mohammad Farrah Aidid. This clan leader, who controlled parts of the south, banned the charcoal trade. But after Aidid's death in 1996, access to the forests fell under the control of various clan factions, whose leaders saw an opportunity to make money. Although the newly formed interim government based in Mogadishu tried to outlaw charcoal exports in September 2001, it met with no success.

Deforestation has had the greatest impact on Somalia's acacia trees, the preferred wood for making charcoal. However, large numbers of other species not typically used to make charcoal, such as mango trees and softwoods, have also been greatly depleted.

Like Somalia's forests, much of its wildlife has also been lost. The country's elephant population is gone, the victim mostly of ivory poachers. Other large animals that used to roam the country, such as giraffes, zebras, oryx (African antelopes), hippopotamuses, and rhinoceroses, have virtually disappeared. Most were killed by hunters for their hides and leather or captured for sale abroad.

Despite encroachments on their habitat, a number of other wild animals live in Somalia, mostly in the less populated regions of the far south. They include foxes, hyenas, leopards, lions, and warthogs. A small antelope known as the **dik-dik** can be found in northern regions. Numerous kinds of birds live in Somalia, including ducks, geese, pelicans, pink flamingos, and ospreys along rivers and coastline; eagles, vultures, hawks, and ravens in mountainous regions; and ostriches in desert savannahs. Snakes commonly found in Somalia include the poisonous puff adder, spitting cobra, and mamba.

> Somalia forms the outer edge of the Horn of Africa, a strategic location for ships traveling from the Indian Ocean to the Mediterranean Sea via the Suez Canal.

With no government oversight of the wildlife populations, statistics on the numbers of animals living in Somalia are hard to come by. Without a strong national government, protection of the remaining wildlife population remains uncertain.

OTHER ENVIRONMENTAL ISSUES

One organization hoping to solve Somalia's environmental problems is the Somali Environmental Protection and Anti-Desertification Organization (SEPADO). Established in 1996, the group monitors and tries to safeguard the environment, particularly by preventing the destruction of the country's limited resources.

Many of Somalia's environmental issues result from its dependence on an agricultural economy. When trees are cut down to make charcoal, or grasses are devastated by overgrazing, the land degrades. In an arid land like Somalia, pastureland can quickly turn into desert.

No strong central government protects Somalia's coastline—from poachers or polluters. Large foreign fishing fleets ply the seas off Somalia's northeastern coast, which, according to **World Bank** studies, is one of the best fishing areas in the world. Fishermen from Somalia's southern coastal towns have actually reported being chased away from favorite fishing spots and having their nets cut by foreign fleets. Each year, SEPADO reports, several thousand tons of dead fish and sea animal carcasses wash ashore in Somalia—apparently poisoned by oil, toxic waste, or other pollutants illegally dumped by tankers passing through the Arabian Sea. In December 2004, nearly 300 Somalis were killed in a tsunami triggered by earthquakes in the Indian Ocean. The tsunami also washed toxic waste ashore, leading to outbreaks of severe stomach, lung, and skin ailments in Somali coastal towns.

SOMALIA'S CAMELS

Pastoral nomads raise and sell cattle, sheep, goats, and camels. But of all the country's domesticated animals, the camel is the most important. In fact, before Somalia's civil war, the country had the largest population of camels in Africa, estimated at 6.5 million. This desert animal can live for extended periods without grass, and it can survive as long as a month without water. Even in extreme heat the camel continues to provide milk, supplying nourishment that keeps its owner alive. The animal serves as transportation for nomads as they travel from one place to the next. And when necessary, the camel is also slaughtered for its meat.

Although Somalia is only Africa's 18th-largest nation, because of its unusual shape it has the continent's second-longest coastline.

Because camels are essential to their survival, Somali nomads have developed a great

In Somalia camels—essential to the survival of nomads but also owned by city dwellers—are a measure of wealth and status, and even the subject of poetry.

respect for these animals. In fact, some Somali poetry, a centuries-old oral tradition, is devoted to the camel, praising its value to the nomad culture.

Camels actually serve as a form of currency for Somalis and are owned by both nomads and city dwellers (who leave their herds in the care of rural relatives). In her autobiography, *Desert Flower*, Somali native Waris Dirie notes that the number of camels a nomad family owns reflects the family's status. Camels are used to pay for wedding dowries and for fines levied for offenses against other clans. Dirie describes how the camel also serves as compensation for murder: "Even a man's life is measured by camels, with one hundred camels being the price for a man who has been killed. A hundred camels must be paid by the killer's clan to the surviving family of the victim, or the dead man's clan will attack the killer in retribution."

A statue of Queen Hatshepsut. In the 15th century B.C., the Egyptian ruler dispatched ships to what is today Somalia. Then called the Land of Punt, or God's Land, it was a place where the resins of two species of trees were collected to produce highly coveted frankincense and myrrh.

History

The history of Somalia dates back thousands of years. Archaeological digs give proof of human occupation as early as A.D. 100. Yet more than 1,000 years earlier, in 1493 B.C., Queen Hatshepsut of Egypt sent ships to the area, known by ancient Greek and Egyptian sailors as the Land of Punt (God's Land). For them it was a holy place, the land to find the fragrant wood, full of frankincense and myrrh resins, burned as incense in religious ceremonies. However, Somalis did not live in the region at the time but came much later.

ORIGINS OF THE SOMALI PEOPLE

Scholars believe that Somalis are descended from two distinct groups—the Cushites and Arab tribes—who eventually merged into the Somali ethnic group. The Cushites came from the Kingdom of Cush, a realm in Sudan that was founded around 1000 B.C. According to the Bible, the kingdom's founder, named Cush, was the first son of Ham, who had migrated to Africa, and the grandson of Noah. By A.D. 1000, descendants of the Kingdom of Cush had migrated south into the Horn of Africa, including parts of modern-day Ethiopia, Djibouti, Somalia, and northern Kenya. Along the way, the Cushites intermarried with members of original African tribes, including the Bantu and Oromo. At the same time, the Cushites took over the northern lands of present-day Somalia.

Arab tribes had established a presence in the Horn of Africa by 1000 as well. Arriving in the 600s as immigrants from Yemen, they had set up the sultanate of Adel on the Gulf of Aden. The sultanate was based in the port city of Zeila, a walled town that became a trading center for coffee and ivory transported from the Abyssinian (Ethiopian) highlands, as well as a market for slaves. Over the next three centuries, Arabs and Persians continued to migrate to Africa, establishing many more trading centers. Some, like Zeila and Berbera, were located in northern Somalia, along the Gulf of Aden. Others, such as Mogadishu, Brava, and Marka, were established in southern Somalia, along the coast of the Indian Ocean.

Many of the Arab settlers who founded clans representing today's Somali family clans, including the Daarood and Isaaq, arrived around 1200. They married local women, including Cushites, and developed a traditional clan structure based upon descendants on the male side. Their clans and others gradually spread out, particularly into the south, including land that is now eastern Ethiopia and northern Kenya. As the Somali ethnic group continued to spread, its members also assimilated with the local African people, the Oromo, through marriage.

Somalis living in the southern part of the country settled down as farmers, while the nomads to the north established migration routes that allowed them to keep their families and herds alive during the dry seasons. Clans laid claim to certain territories within their migration area, controlling access to the water holes.

When the Arab tribes came to Africa, they brought their Islamic faith with them. Islam—whose founding, by the prophet Muhammad, is dated to A.D. 622—was first introduced to Somalia by Muhammad's followers. They arrived during the 700s, and the Islamic faith quickly spread from the coastal regions to the interior, displacing Christianity and other local religions. By the 13th century, virtually all ethnic Somalis followed the Islamic faith.

From the 13th to 16th centuries, Somalis fought in regional wars between Christians and Muslims. During the 15th century, Somali Muslims (as followers of Islam are called) invaded the Ogaden region, then part of the kingdom of Abyssinia (present-day Ethiopia). After an Abyssinian leader named Yeshaq defeated a Somali town, he directed his supporters to compose a victory hymn. That song, written in 1415, became one of the first written records to mention the Somalis.

By the end of the 16th century, Arab control of the Indian Ocean trading network had waned, and the sultanate of Adel had disintegrated into small independent territories. Many were ruled by the leaders of Somali clans.

EUROPEAN RULE

In the 1800s several European powers developed an interest in Somalia because it lay on the shipping route to India and Indochina. In 1839 Great Britain annexed Aden, across the sea from Somalia, in the present-day Republic of Yemen. The site let the British navy protect the country's trade routes and provided safe anchorage for merchant ships. About 50 years later, Britain took control of the Somalian cities of Zeila and Berbera, to safeguard the route to India through the Suez Canal, which had opened in 1869.

The United Kingdom regarded northern Somalia mainly as a source of livestock for Aden, which had become a principal supply post for British ships traveling to India through the Suez Canal. Toward the end of the 1800s, the British government made treaties with Somali leaders in northern Somalia and with the Ethiopian king, Menelik I. In 1896 the boundaries of a protectorate called British Somaliland were established.

Around the same time, Italy had developed an interest in Indian Ocean outposts along Somalia's eastern coast. The Italians concluded agreements with the local Somali sultans of Obbia and Aluula, who placed their land under the protection of Italy. Between 1897 and 1908, Italy signed several treaties with Ethiopia and England, establishing boundaries for its own protectorate, known as Italian Somaliland.

This engraving depicts Menelik I with his chiefs. The Ethiopian king compelled Italy and Great Britain to recognize his country's claims to the Haud and Ogaden regions, parts of which Somalia and Ethiopia continue to contest today.

By the beginning of the 20th century other countries had laid claim to lands where Somali people lived. King Menelik of Ethiopia, who defeated the Italian army at the Battle of Adwa in 1896, forced Italy and Britain to recognize his country's claims to the Haud and Ogaden regions. Kenya controlled land on its northern border that was inhabited by Somalis. And a third European power, France, ruled a small colony in Djibouti, on Somalia's northwestern border.

Some Somalis challenged this colonial control. One of the strongest resistance movements came from dervishes, devout members of the Islamic Sufi mystical sect. From 1899 to 1920 their leader, Mohammed ibn Abdullah Hassan, led multitudes of his disciples into battle against the Ethiopians and the British.

Somalis held the Muslim leader, known as "the Sayyid," in great respect. The British, on the other hand, considered him to be little more than a religious fanatic, calling him "the Mad Mullah." But his followers fought doggedly. In 1910 they forced the British to withdraw from the interior to the coast of the protectorate. During World War I the Germans and Turks sided with Abdullah, but in 1920 British warplanes bombed his camp in northern Somalia, forcing him to flee. He died from natural causes later that year.

Abdullah's 20 years of fighting failed to earn freedom for his country, and about one-third of the population of northern Somalia and the Ogaden died as a result of the struggle. Nevertheless, the determined Muslim leader is celebrated today as a national hero.

During the 1920s, Italian colonial occupation gradually extended inland from the Indian Ocean coast. Italy acquired a portion of the Jubaland Province of Kenya, which included the port of Kismaayo, from the British, and took over the independent sultanates of Obbia and Mijertein. Then Italian forces moved into the Ogaden region of eastern Ethiopia and captured its capital, Addis Ababa. In 1936 Italy annexed Ethiopia and merged it with Italian Somaliland and Eritrea to form Italian East Africa.

SEEKING INDEPENDENCE

In 1940 the government of Italy entered World War II (1939–45) on the side of Germany. That August, Italian forces invaded British Somaliland and drove out the British. A year later, however, English troops retook the protectorate and conquered Italian Somaliland and the Ogaden.

The British placed all three areas under military administration, with Hargeysa as the capital, and governed the entire region until 1950. That year the United Nations General Assembly determined that Italy should govern the former Italian Somaliland as a U.N. trust territory, and after 10 years of this provisional administration, the region would be granted independence.

The British remained in control of northern Somalia and continued in efforts to improve the judicial, educational, and health system for Somalis. For the first time, Somalis participated in their government as clerks in local courts and as members of government planning and advisory committees. Somalia's first political party, the Somali Youth League, was established in the 1940s, and elections for a legislative assembly were held in 1960. One of the first acts of the assembly was to request that British Somaliland be granted independence from the United Kingdom so it could unite with Italian Somaliland.

The British government complied on June 26, 1960, granting British Somaliland its independence. A few days later, on July 1, Italian Somaliland also gained its independence and merged with the former British protectorate to form the Republic of Somalia. Mogadishu was selected as the new nation's capital.

Disagreements soon arose over what course the Somalian government should take. Pro-Arab and **Pan-Somali** militants wished to unite with the parts of Kenya and Ethiopia where other Somalis lived. Reformers wanted to address economic and social development issues, as well as improve relations with other African countries. Political parties were based on clan affiliation, which resulted in a divergence of interests between northern and southern leaders.

In June 1961, Somali voters approved a national referendum and adopted the country's first national constitution. It provided for a democratic state with an elected national assembly. The first elected president of Somalia was Aden Abdullah Osman, and the first prime minister was Abdi Rashid Ali Shermarke.

During the national assembly elections, held in 1964, President Osman appointed a new cabinet, replacing Prime Minister Shermarke with Abdirazak Haji Hussein. In response to this political rebuff, Shermarke decided to oppose Osman in the 1967 elections for the presidency. Shermarke won, and when he was sworn in as president that year, the event marked the first peaceful transfer of power to take place in Africa. Shermarke appointed Mohammed Ibrahim Egal as Somalia's new prime minister. During the next two years Egal improved relations with Kenya and Ethiopia. But the young government did not last much longer.

THE REGIME OF SIAD BARRE

On October 15, 1969, President Shermarke was shot and killed by one of his bodyguards. Six days later, on October 21, 1969, Major General Mohamed Siad Barre assumed power in a bloodless military coup. Siad Barre replaced the country's freely elected National Assembly with the Supreme Revolutionary Council, a military junta he headed as president.

Under Siad Barre, the nation was renamed the Somali Democratic Republic, but the country was a dictatorship. All political parties were banned, political opponents were arrested and sometimes executed, and information and the media were strictly controlled. In 1970 Somalia was declared a socialist state, and the government took over many businesses. Somalia's government allied itself closely with the Soviet Union. In 1974 the two countries signed a joint treaty of friendship and cooperation.

Siad Barre's modernization campaign made some progress. He solicited foreign investment and loans for public works projects, such as port renovations and road improvements. His government set up agricultural cooperatives, creating large state farms in which farmers shared the work. And in 1972 his Language Commission developed a system of writing in Somali, which until then had been only an oral language.

Siad Barre also held strong pan-Somali views, believing that Somalia should be united with all Somali-inhabited territories. In July 1977 the Somali National Army joined a faction of ethnic rebels who crossed into the Ogaden region of Ethiopia with plans to gain control of the often-contested area. By late 1977, Somalia had

In October 1969, Mohamed Siad Barre assumed power in Somalia in a bloodless coup. Although he undertook a campaign to modernize the country, the former army general ruled with an iron fist. He was finally ousted in 1991.

captured most of the region, but then its former ally, the Soviet Union, sided with Ethiopia, providing arms and troops to resist the Somalian invasion.

By early 1978, Ethiopia had regained its territory, and Siad Barre had severed all relations with the Soviet Union. Although the Ogaden War lasted only a year, Somalia's army suffered heavy losses, and the country had to absorb 400,000 refugees who fled from Ethiopia into Somalia. Subsequent drought and famine drove the total number of homeless to 2 million as of 1981. Siad Barre turned to the Western powers for help, allowing U.S. forces to establish military facilities in Somalia in exchange for millions of dollars in humanitarian assistance, economic development, and military aid.

Although Siad Barre enjoyed some popular support during the early years of his rule, by the late 1970s his regime had become increasingly oppressive. As a result, a growing number of clan-based political factions developed with the goal of overthrowing the government. Organizers of a failed coup in 1978 fled to Ethiopia, where they formed the rebel Somali Salvation Democratic Front (SSDF). The SSDF, which comprised the Majeerteen subclan of the Daarood, developed a strong following in central and northeastern Somalia.

In response, Siad Barre imprisoned some Majeerteen military and civilian leaders. He gave government positions only to those he thought would remain loyal—members of his own family subclan, the Daarood Mareehaan, and the related Dulbahante and Ogaden subclans. For the next several years he attempted to maintain control and divert attention from the problems of his increasingly unpopular regime by pitting clans against one another.

A CATASTROPHIC CIVIL WAR

In the early 1980s the SSDF initiated a series of attacks on Siad Barre's regime and was joined by another political faction, the

Somali National Movement (SNM), which was made up mostly of members of the northwestern Isaaq clan. Periodic clashes between government troops and these factions, which were aided by forces from Ethiopia, erupted into open civil war in 1988, when Siad Barre ordered a campaign against northern Somalia.

Angry over the northern population's apparent support for the SNM, Siad Barre ordered the destruction of city pumping systems, the poisoning of rural wells, and the machine-gunning of livestock herds. In May 1988 the Somali National Air Force bombed northern cities indiscriminately, flattening Hargeysa and Burao. The death toll in Hargeysa alone reached 50,000. Hundreds of thousands of civilians fled to Ethiopia.

Determined to oust Siad Barre from power, other anti-government factions formed. Members of the Hawiye clan made up the United Somali Congress (USC), which battled government forces in central Somalia. The Somali Patriotic Movement (SPM), consisting of members of the Daarood-Ogaden subclan, operated around the Jubba River Basin.

In December 1990, USC forces entered Mogadishu. Soon fierce fighting broke out between the USC and Siad Barre's elite military unit, the Red Berets, commanded by the dictator's oldest son. As the situation deteriorated, the U.S. government dispatched helicopters to Mogadishu on January 5, 1991, to rescue Americans and other foreigners from the U.S. embassy. After four weeks of street battles, the USC defeated Siad Barre's forces, and on January 27, 1991, the dictator and his supporters fled the capital. Siad Barre later died of a heart attack while in exile in Lagos, Nigeria.

The USC quickly established a provisional government, naming Ali Mahdi Muhammad as interim president. However, a USC general named Mohammad Farrah Aidid rejected this choice. Once again fighting raged in Mogadishu, as militias loyal to the rival USC leaders battled each another.

Within other clans and subclans as well, rivalries escalated to street fighting in the capital and elsewhere around the country, as various factions battled for territory and political power. The collapse of the Somalian government meant the end to the Somali National Army. Clan militiamen and bandits laid claim to the army's military equipment and looted government buildings, schools, shops, and homes. Indiscriminate violence spread throughout southern Somalia, as death squads hunted down and executed members of rival clans. By the end of 1991, civilian deaths in Mogadishu alone reached 14,000. Somalia lost most of its commercial and farming communities as more than 700,000 Somalis fled the country.

On May 18, 1991, the northwestern region of Somalia, dominated by the Isaaq clan and its Somali National Movement, officially broke away from the rest of the country. It declared its independence as the new nation of Somaliland, claiming the same boundaries as the former protectorate of British Somaliland. The new Somaliland government named Hargeysa as its capital.

Compounding the disaster of war and political turmoil, a prolonged drought in 1992 brought on a severe famine in southern Somalia. Weakened by hunger and malnutrition, rural Somalis left their homes for refugee camps in hopes of finding food. The U.N. estimated that 1.5 million Somalis were in imminent danger of starvation as a result of famine and civil war.

International relief agencies tried to provide food and medical aid, but clan factions stole as much as 80 percent of the supplies intended for the needy. At airports and seaports, gangs of armed profiteers demanded money and a share of the relief agency shipments. In August 1992 the U.N. voted to send an armed peacekeeping force to Somalia. Their mission was to restore order so that relief agencies could effectively help the starving people of the country.

OPERATION RESTORE HOPE

On December 9, 1992, the U.S. contingent of the U.N. peace-keeping force entered Somalia as part of Operation Restore Hope. Under the protection of the peacekeepers, international agencies soon resumed food distribution and other humanitarian aid.

The U.N. presence in Mogadishu was strongly opposed by warlord Mohammad Farrah Aidid, the USC general who also headed an armed political faction called the Somali National Alliance (SNA). The SNA, made up of the Hawiye–Habar Gidir subclan, controlled much of Mogadishu.

In June 1993, members of the SNA murdered 24 Pakistani peacekeeping soldiers in Mogadishu. Calling the SNA a major threat to rebuilding a government in Somalia, the U.N. approved attacks against Aidid and his SNA. In July, U.S. forces mistakenly attacked a Habar Gidir clan meeting, killing more than 50 unarmed Somalis. In the wake of the assault, Somali hostility toward the international forces, and specifically toward the American contingent, grew.

The following October, U.S. troops attempted to capture Aidid's military aides in Mogadishu. At the beginning of the assault, two Black Hawk helicopters were shot down by Somali fighters. During the ensuing 17-hour battle, 18 Americans—members of elite units of the U.S. Army's Rangers and Delta Force—were killed and 84 were wounded. Hundreds of Somalis perished as well. Americans were horrified to see news footage showing cheering Somalis dragging the body of a dead U.S. pilot through Mogadishu's streets. The operation was recounted in Mark Bowden's 1999 book, *Black Hawk Down*, and depicted in a 2001 movie of the same name.

U.S. troops were withdrawn in March 1994, but returned the following February to assist in the evacuation of the remaining U.N. peacekeeping forces. Although Operation Restore Hope failed to

Somali warlords Mohammad Farrah Aidid (left) and Ali Mahdi Muhammad shake hands to signal a truce between their rival factions, December 12, 1992. The agreement was soon broken as Aidid and Muhammad resumed their struggle for power.

restore peace to Somalia, the international relief effort did save an estimated 300,000 Somalis from starvation.

In June 1995 Aidid declared himself president of the country. However, rival clans refused to recognize his claim, and battles for control of Somalia resumed. A year later, Aidid died from wounds received during a fight. He was replaced by his son Hussein Mohammad Aidid.

A FRAGILE GOVERNMENT

Sporadic clashes between warring factions continued after 1995, although a series of cease-fires brought peace for short intervals in late 1996 and 1997. In 1998 the Somali Salvation Democratic Front (SSDF), the major faction in northeastern Somalia, announced the creation of an autonomous state called Puntland. The region had already seen years of civil unrest, beginning in 1991, with fighting between the SSDF and Islamic fundamentalists.

After at least 13 failed attempts at making peace throughout the 1990s, a reconciliation conference begun in May 2000 finally made

Somali children atop the wreckage of one of two U.S. Black Hawk helicopters shot down during the Battle of Mogadishu. Eighteen American servicemen and as many as 500 Somalis died in the fierce firefight, which broke out on October 3, 1993, when U.S. troops supporting a United Nations humanitarian mission attempted to seize aides to warlord Mohammad Farrah Aidid.

some progress. Held in the town of Arta, Djibouti, the conference included clan elders, leaders of armed and unarmed political factions, and members of human rights, women's, and minority groups. No representatives from Somaliland or Puntland attended, nor did four warlords based in Mogadishu.

By July the conference members had agreed to establish a Transitional National Government (TNG) for Somalia. The transitional parliament elected an interim president, Abdulkassim Salat Hassan, who made Ali Khalif Galaydh prime minister. The entire TNG cabinet was replaced in late 2001, and a new prime minister,

Hassan Abshir Farah, was appointed. The new government immediately faced fierce opposition from warlords and sect leaders.

In 2002 a third breakaway region, in and around the town of Baidoa (near the disputed Ogaden border with Ethiopia), announced plans to secede from Somalia. The Rahanwayn Resistance Army (RRA), a political faction of the Rahanwayn clan, declared that the new government would be called the State of Southwestern Somalia. By 2006, the RRA seemed to have postponed its goal of autonomy.

By August 2004, warring factions agreed to join a reformed transitional parliament and were inaugurated in Eldoret, Kenya. Abdullahi Yusuf became president of the new Transitional Federal Government (TFG). The TFG gained recognition and support from the United Nations and many African neighbors, but bitter divisions remained. Cabinet members were often attacked, and the TFG could not find a safe, neutral meeting place. Yet another parliament reorganization took place in January 2006.

In June 2006, the Islamic Courts Union (ICU), a group of southern clan leaders organized into militias, attacked warlords and TFG strongholds to conquer much of southern Somalia, including Mogadishu. The ICU imposed fundamentalist Islamism on the occupied areas. With the backing of Ethiopian troops, the TFG overthrew the ICU in much of the country by early 2007. Moderate ICU members joined the TFG (a moderate Islamist, Sheikh Sharif Sheikh Ahmed, became president of Somalia in 2008), but hardline supporters formed new insurgency groups, the largest of which called itself al-Shabaab. As of 2009, the TFG had only gained control of small areas of Mogadishu, and hundreds of civilians had died in power struggles with warlords and insurgents.

Somalis outside an al-Barakaat office in Mogadishu. Among other enterprises, al-Barakaat operates a money-transfer service that enables Somalis living and working abroad to send funds to relatives in Somalia. In an economy decimated by years of drought, famine, and civil war, these remittances are the largest single source of income.

The Economy, Politics, and Religion

Somalia is one of the poorest and least developed countries in the world. For most Somalis, who are engaged in subsistence agriculture—producing barely enough to sustain their families—survival is a daily struggle.

ECONOMIC OVERVIEW

Because Somalia lacks a functioning central government and a national financial authority, the overall health of the country's economy is difficult to measure. Standard economic indicators, such as **gross domestic product (GDP)** and inflation rate, are unreliable because little dependable data exists upon which to base estimates.

What is known is that Somalia was poor even before civil war broke out. In the late 1980s the GDP per capita—the value of all goods and services produced in the country per person—

was estimated at just $290. That's less than one dollar per person per day. By the early 1990s GDP per capita had fallen drastically, to $36, or just 10¢ per person per day. As of 2008, the figure had risen to an estimated $600, but that still placed Somalia among the world's low-income nations.

Somalia's single largest source of income is money sent home by Somalis living and working abroad, of whom there are more than 1 million. These funds, called **remittances**, help Somali families buy food or clothing or support their small businesses. Sometimes, overseas workers send manufactured goods instead of money to their families. Estimates of the money shipped back home to Somalia each year range from $500 million to $750 million.

Economists cannot precisely determine Somalia's annual rate of inflation—the increasing cost of goods over time—but estimate it at well over 100 percent, meaning that the same amount of money will be worth less than half as much in a year. Somalia's inflation is uncontrolled because the country's national currency, the **Somali shilling**, is printed not by a federal government but by Somali businesses. As the number of bills in circulation rises, the value of the shilling falls, creating an inflationary spiral.

Traditionally the agriculture sector has contributed the most to Somalia's economy, accounting for about two-thirds of the country's GDP. However, bad weather can wreak havoc on agricultural and livestock production. Several years of low rainfall in the late 1990s and early 2000 made Somalis increasingly dependent on remittances from overseas workers.

Before the war, about 85 percent of Somalia's workforce was engaged in some form of agriculture (25 percent as settled farmers, 60 percent as pastoral nomads). By 2001 the proportion of agricultural workers had fallen to about 70 percent; about 30 percent of Somali workers had jobs in industry and services—for example, as government employees, factory workers, or merchants.

Somalia's flag was designed in the 1950s, when the country was administered by Italy as a United Nations trust territory. The colors mirror those of the U.N. flag, with the white star representing peace and prosperity.

AGRICULTURE, FORESTRY, AND FISHING

Fertile plantations in southern Somalia, near the Jubba and Shabeelle Rivers, produce bananas, mangoes, papayas, and sugarcane. In certain areas of the Ogo highlands and along the ocean coast, farmers raise corn, cotton, and sorghum. Although about 13 percent of Somalia's land is considered suitable for farming, only about 2 percent of it is actually cultivated.

Until recently Somalia's major agricultural export was livestock, accounting for about 40 percent of the country's GDP. For many years camels, cattle, sheep, and goats were raised for domestic use and export, with Saudi Arabia as a major market. However, toward the end of 2000, Saudi Arabia and other Persian Gulf states banned the import of Somalian livestock because of fears the animals carried an infectious disease called Rift Valley fever.

The ban resulted in a significant loss of income for many Somalis. They could no longer sell their livestock overseas, and the

A Somali woman shops for charcoal at a market in Mogadishu. Despite the environmental devastation that charcoal production has wrought, charcoal is still widely used by Somalis for cooking and heating, and it is one of the country's major export products.

decrease in exports meant an increase in the number of animals offered for sale locally. This oversupply caused selling prices to plummet. In mid-2002, the United Arab Emirates lifted its ban, but since the UAE accounts for only about 2 percent of Somalian live-stock exported to countries in the Arabian Peninsula, that action had only a minor impact.

An important Somalian forestry export comes from its incense trees, the *Boswellia* and *Commiphora*, which supply resins of frank-incense and myrrh. Harvesting the resins does not require killing the trees. Somalis slash the bark just enough to make it bleed a milky fluid, which eventually hardens into clumps of gum that are collected and sold.

Charcoal has also become a major export, despite the massive deforestation this has caused. Because of the livestock ban, many Somalis have resorted to making money by cutting trees and turning the wood into charcoal (by burying and then slowly burning it). Most of the charcoal is sold locally, but a significant amount is exported. According to some authorities, charcoal has surpassed bananas among Somalia's major exports.

Despite its extensive coastline, Somalia has only a small fishing industry. Overfishing and pollution have depleted Somalia's stock of warm-water fish. A number of Somalis who once made their living from fishing have turned to piracy.

INDUSTRY

Before the central government failed in the early 1990s, Somalia had enjoyed a small amount of industrial growth and development. Although some factories still function, many have closed, their parts looted and sold for scrap.

Light industries include meat, milk, and fish processing; sugar refining; and fruit and vegetable canning. Other businesses include textile manufacturers and tanneries, which process animal hides and skins to produce leather. The country's only oil refinery, located in Mogadishu, has been out of operation since the war.

Somalia has a very small mining industry, which extracts mostly salt and gypsum. Deposits of iron ore, uranium, beryl, columbite, tin, and bauxite have been discovered but are not mined. The country may also have significant reserves of petroleum and natural gas in the northern regions, but they have not been developed because of the ongoing political turmoil.

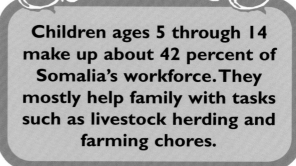

Children ages 5 through 14 make up about 42 percent of Somalia's workforce. They mostly help family with tasks such as livestock herding and farming chores.

The contribution of manufacturing to Somalia's economy is low, estimated at just 10 percent of the GDP.

SERVICES

The services sector of Somalia's economy provided 25 percent of the country's GDP in 2000. The strongest components are the telecommunications industry and money transfer services.

In the early 1990s Somalia had just one tiny public telephone service, in Mogadishu. It was virtually destroyed by looters who stole lines of copper telephone wires and other parts for sale overseas. Ten years later, however, a thriving new telecommunications industry was in place. With a presence in most urban areas, the growing industry provides cellular mobile service, public telephones, and Internet services.

Money transfer services have benefited from the relocation of so many Somalis to other countries. Found in large and small towns throughout Somalia, these services follow the **hawala** system, an alternative to formal banking used in the Muslim world to transfer money overseas. Money deliveries can be made quickly and efficiently, even in areas without banks, although the system has no legal backing or status.

The *hawalas* are based on complicated clan connections that have been established over the years. Transactions rely on trust. A Somali living abroad contacts and gives money to the *hawala* dealer, agreeing to pay a 5 percent commission. The overseas *hawala* dealer calls or e-mails a corresponding dealer based in Somalia. The Somali *hawala* dealer then delivers the money, knowing he will be reimbursed from elsewhere within the international *hawala* system.

FOREIGN TRADE

Somalia's major exports—livestock, bananas, charcoal, animal hides and skins, fish and fish products, and myrrh—all come from the agricultural sector. The bulk of these goods are shipped to Saudi Arabia, Yemen, the United Arab Emirates, Italy, and Pakistan.

Somalia imports a great deal of its food, particularly food grains (wheat and rice) and animal and vegetable oils. International food aid has provided additional cereal grains in times of famine.

Other major imports include petroleum products, transportation equipment, non-electrical machinery, construction materials, iron and steel, textiles, and a leaf called khat (or qat) that, when chewed, produces a mildly stimulating effect. These imports come mainly from Djibouti, Kenya, Brazil, Saudi Arabia, and India.

A Somali youth displays a bag of fresh khat. Most Somali men chew the leaf, which produces a mildly stimulating effect.

Most Somali men chew the leaf of the *Catha edulis* bush, known as khat, which is imported from Kenya. To have the desired effect, the leaf must be green. Daily flights take off at dawn from Nairobi with shipments of fresh khat. The leaves were picked the night before, from bushes growing in Kenya's Meru Mountains, and then trucked to the capital for the morning flight to Somalia. Khat is legal in both Kenya and Somalia, and the drug flights bringing the product often provide airline services as well.

ENERGY AND TRANSPORTATION

Somalia relies on wood, charcoal, and imported petroleum to meet its energy needs. Only Mogadishu and a few towns have electricity. Power is provided by electrical generators that run on diesel fuel. However, oil must be imported, and deliveries have been unreliable and increasingly expensive.

All transportation systems in Somalia are in need of improvement. There are no railways connecting major cities and towns—the only one was destroyed during World War II. Of the approximately 14,000 miles (22,500 km) of roads in the country, only about one-quarter are paved or gravel. Most have had little maintenance and are in disrepair; some are even riddled with land mines. During the rainy seasons the dirt roads become impassable, even to four-wheel drive pickups and other off-road vehicles.

Somalia's only international airport, located in Mogadishu, was shut down in 1995 because of the civil war. There are about 100 airstrips throughout the country, but most are little more than dirt runways. (At least five warlords control various dirt landing strips in Mogadishu.) Charter airlines provide some air transportation to Mogadishu and other parts of Somalia. Private airlines, such as Air Somalia and Daallo Airlines, operate from the Hargeysa airport or other small airports in Berbera and Bossaso.

COMMUNICATIONS

Several Mogadishu-based radio stations operate in Somalia, including Radio Mogadishu, Voice of the Republic of Somalia (operated by the transitional government), as well as stations supporting various factions. The government of breakaway Somaliland operates Radio Hargeysa, while the Puntland regional government broadcasts Radio Gaalkacyo.

Somalia has a handful of daily newspapers, the most important of which are published in Mogadishu. Somaliland and Puntland also have their own newspapers. News services on the Internet include the Somali Press Online and Somali News Online.

Two independent television stations broadcast in Somalia: Somali Television Network (STN), which broadcasts Qatar-based Al-Jazeera TV, and HornAfrik.

FOREIGN AND HUMANITARIAN AID

During the 1960s and 1970s, Somalia depended on aid from the Soviet Union to fund infrastructure improvement and economic development projects. After breaking ties with the Soviet Union in 1978, Somalia borrowed from the United States and other Western nations, through the World Bank and **International Monetary Fund** (IMF). Unable to repay these loans, Somalia accumulated a massive foreign debt (estimated in 2001 at $3 billion, or more than 60 percent of the country's GDP). As a result, most countries are reluctant to give loans to Somalia, especially in the absence of an effective national government.

However, Somalia continues to receive funding, food, and medical services through a number of humanitarian groups. As of 2008, about 40 international and local aid agencies were operating in the country. However, these aid groups are sometimes forced to withdraw their workers due to fighting between Islamist militants and government troops. Aid is distributed by the Somali Support Secretariat, an organization made up of United Nations agencies, nongovernmental organizations, and donors. Primary donors include the European Union, the United States, and the African Union.

In April 2009, a relief agency estimated that over 40 percent of Somalia's people depended on aid groups for food. However, constant violence hinders these groups from operating. Workers are often taken hostage. Along the coast, ships containing food and

The Economy of Somalia

Gross domestic product (GDP*): $5.524 billion

GDP per capita: $600

Inflation: cannot be determined (business print their own money)

Natural resources: uranium and largely untapped reserves of iron ore, tin, gypsum, bauxite, copper, and salt; potential oil and natural gas reserves

Agriculture (65% of GDP): livestock; bananas, sorghum, corn, sugarcane, mangoes, sesame seeds, beans, fish, rice; hides; charcoal (2000 est.)

Industry (10% of GDP): a few light industries, including processed foods and sugar refining, textiles, petroleum refining (mostly shut down), wireless communications (2000 est.)

Services (25% of GDP): telecommunications, money transfer services, hotels, retail markets (2000 est.)

Foreign trade:

Imports—$798 million: manufactured items, petroleum products, food, construction material, khat (2006 est.)

Exports—$300 million: livestock, bananas, charcoal, hides, fish, scrap metal (2006 est.)

Currency exchange rate: 1,406.38 Somali shillings = U.S. $1 (May 2009) (Somaliland issues its own currency, the Somaliland shilling, which is not recognized by foreign countries)

*GDP, or gross domestic product, is the total value of goods and services produced in a country annually. Note: Due to the lack of a permanent national government, most statistical data on Somalia is estimated and may not be accurate. Figures are 2008 estimates unless otherwise indicated. Sources: CIA World Factbook, 2009; U.S. Department of State; Bloomberg.com.

emergency relief supplies are frequent targets of pirates. According to 2007 U.N. statistics, about 1.1 million Somalis are internally displaced persons and more than 450,000 are refugees.

POLITICS AND GOVERNMENT

In recent decades, three clans—the Isaaq, Daarood, and Hawiye—have had the greatest impact on Somalia, by physically dividing the country up. The Isaaq clan–based Somali National Movement formed the Republic of Somaliland in northwestern Somalia. In central and northeastern Somalia, the Harti subclan of the Daarood established Puntland. In the south, members of the Hawiye-Habar Gidir, who make up the United Somali Congress/Somali National Alliance, developed strongholds in Mogadishu.

Approximately 30 clan-based factions continue to vie for power throughout the country. Their bitter, ongoing feuds make the establishment of a stable, united Somalia a difficult challenge.

Although the Somali Transitional Federal Government is trying to unite the country, it has had little success. Set up to operate like an official national government, the TFG consists of an executive branch with a president, a prime minister, and a 36-member cabinet, as well as a unicameral (one-house) legislature, the 550-member Transitional Federal Assembly. There is no national judicial court. The transitional government was established in August 2000, in the town of Arta, Djibouti, but moved to the Somalian capital of Mogadishu in October 2000.

Because Somalia lacks a central judicial court, Somalis have turned to secular clan leaders and to Muslim clerics versed in *Sharia*, or Islamic religious law, to settle local issues and disputes. In some cases, *Sharia* courts have their own militia to protect the clerics. Today the Islamic courts have considerable influence throughout Somalia, even though secular clan leaders and warlords effectively rule the country.

SOMALILAND AND PUNTLAND GOVERNMENTS

Since proclaiming its independence on May 16, 1991, Somaliland has established a government consisting of an executive branch, headed by a president who serves for a term of five years; a bicameral parliament made up of an elders chamber and a house of representatives; and an independent judiciary. The voting age is 18, for men and women.

No political parties were allowed in Somaliland until June 2000, when the parliament passed a law permitting the formation of three political parties. Local elections were held the following year, and at that time Somaliland voters overwhelmingly endorsed the move to independence from Somalia by approving Somaliland's new constitution. In 1993 the former prime minister of the Somali Republic, Mohammed Ibrahim Egal, was elected president of the breakaway nation. Egal died in May 2002, during his second term in office, and his position was filled by Vice President Dahir Riyale Kahin.

Although Somaliland has established its own currency and had some success in obtaining foreign aid for various development and infrastructure projects, it has not been recognized as an independent nation by the international community. Without such recognition, Somaliland cannot establish trade agreements with other countries or receive loans from the IMF or World Bank. The Somali Transitional National Government opposes Somaliland's claim to independence.

Puntland has not declared independence from Somalia, although the northeastern region's dominant political faction, the Somali Salvation Democratic Front (SSDF), set up a separate regional government in 1998. At the time, Puntland's leaders claimed they were forming an autonomous state that would reunite with Somalia when a true national government was established.

With Garowe its capital and SSDF leader Abdullahi Yusuf Ahmed

Mohammed Ibrahim Egal, president of the breakaway Republic of Somaliland, shakes hands with supporters during a May 2001 constitutional referendum. Although voters overwhelmingly endorsed complete independence from Somalia, the international community does not recognize Somaliland as a sovereign nation.

as its president, Puntland set up operations, with the plan to restore order, helped by the institution of military and police forces. Then, in November 2001, a convention of elders chose Colonel Jama Ali Maji as president. In response, forces loyal to former president Abdullahi Yusuf Ahmed attacked Garowe. Government control was shaken by this conflict, and by subsequent clashes among other factions vying for authority in the region. By the end of 2002, Abdullahi Yusuf Ahmed had returned to power as president. He remained in the office until 2004, when he began four years as president of Somalia's Transitional Federal Government.

RELIGION: THE ISLAMIC FAITH

Almost all Somalis are Sunni Muslims, followers of the Islamic faith's dominant branch. Islam structures not only the spiritual life, but also the political, social, and moral life, of believers. Islam is based on the teachings of the prophet Muhammad, as they appear in the Islamic holy book, the **Qur'an** (also spelled Koran). Muslims also follow the **hadith**, which describes Muhammad's actions and traditional sayings. Together, the Qur'an and the hadith form the *Sunna*, the guide for orthodox, or Sunni, Muslims.

The basic tenet of Islam states that there is only one God, Allah, and that Muhammad is His prophet. Muslims must abide by the five "pillars" of Islam: the profession of faith, daily prayers, fasting during the month of Ramadan, giving alms, and the pilgrimage to Mecca, in Saudi Arabia. Islamic religious law, or *Sharia*, governs Muslim behavior. *Sharia* defines actions as mandatory (such as following the five pillars of the faith), recommended (such as nightlong prayer), indifferent (ordinary secular activities), objectionable but not forbidden (divorce), or prohibited (adultery).

Upon becoming an independent nation in 1960, Somalia established Islam as the state religion. Until the civil war, boys attended schools or mosques in cities, where they studied the Qur'an. In rural areas, boys learned from traveling teachers, who accompanied nomadic groups in their journeys over Somalia's savannahs and deserts. Besides providing religious instruction, these teachers also led the tribes in prayer, blessed the people and their livestock, settled disputes, and performed marriages. If they had no traveling teachers, nomads looked to the *wadad*, a literate clan member who

A page from the Qur'an, Islam's holy book. More than 99 percent of Somalia's people are Sunni Muslims.

provided instruction and served as an authority on religious law.

During its brief takeover of Mogadishu, the Islamic Courts Union strictly enforced *Sharia*. Women were kept from going to work. Somalis reported being harassed and beaten for such perceived offenses as throwing parties, playing music, or wearing clothing deemed immodest. Suspected criminals were flogged, mutilated, and sometimes executed in public. Under this harsh regime, street crime declined for the first time in decades, and necessities such as food became more available.

Although most Somalis are not sympathetic to radical Islamic views, many came to believe that Islamist rule could stabilize Somalia. In 2009, Somalia's transitional parliament voted to adopt *Sharia*, hoping to make Islamist organizations irrelevant. Still, al-Shabaab and other groups continued taking control of large areas. Civilians remained torn between their distrust of religious extremism and their need for security.

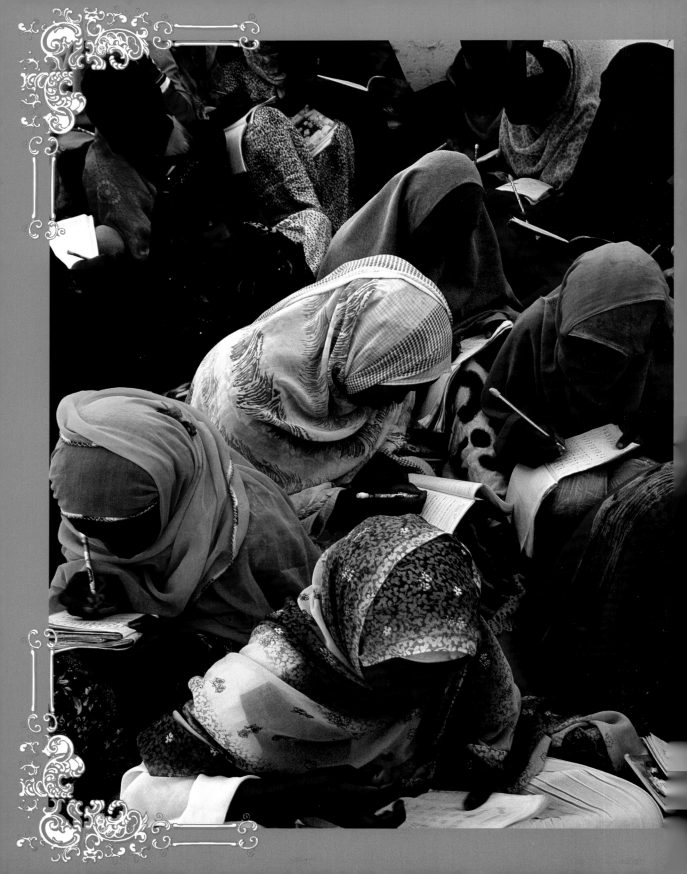

Somali women at an outdoor literacy class. Today, fewer than 4 in 10 Somalis age 15 and older can read and write, and even basic education for their children is beyond the means of most Somali families.

The People

Of the more than 9 million people living in Somalia, about 85 percent are ethnic Somalis. Other ethnic groups include people of Swahili and Bantu descent, who live mostly in farming villages and towns in central and southern Somalia. Some coastal towns, such as Brava, Marka, and Mogadishu, contain descendants of Arabs, Indians, Italians, and Pakistanis. Minority groups include urban coastal peoples (Benadiri or Rer Hamar), craftsmen groups (Midgan, Tumal, Yibir), and fishing people who live along the coast (Bajuni).

LANGUAGE AND EDUCATION

The official language of Somalia is Somali. Arabic is the language of the Islamic faith. In addition, English is spoken in the northern areas, Italian in the south, and Swahili in coastal areas near Kenya. Because Somali was only an oral language until the early 1970s, English and Italian served as the written languages of government and education, while Arabic was used for religious purposes.

In 1972 a newly developed Somali script, based on the Roman alphabet, was developed as part of President Mohamed Siad Barre's modernization program. The following year the Supreme Revolutionary Council established it as the nation's official language and soon afterward launched an intensive literacy campaign. The goal was to teach everyone how to read and write in the new script. Even nomadic pastoralists received instruction—though in outdoor classrooms so they could still watch over their herds. Under Siad Barre's regime, education was free and mandatory for children ages 6 to 14. The literacy campaign proved effective, raising Somalia's literacy rate from 5 percent of the population in the early 1970s to about 24 percent by 1990.

But education is one of the many systems that collapsed when Siad Barre's government fell apart. In the years of anarchy that followed, schools were destroyed as armed thugs looted books, equipment, furniture, and other supplies. Hundreds of schools closed, including the country's only college, the Somali National University, located in Mogadishu.

> In 2002 it cost $6 a month to attend the Al Islah primary and secondary schools and $600 a year to attend the university in Mogadishu. This tuition is out of the reach of most Somalis, who make on average less than a dollar a day.

Although the days of free and compulsory education have ended, it is still possible to attend school in Somalia—for those who can afford the fees. Since 1991 some new universities have opened, including Amoud University, in Borama; the University of Hargeysa; East Africa University, in Bossaso; and Benadir University, in Mogadishu.

Somalia is almost as large as Texas but has less than 40 percent of that U.S. state's population. Somalia's population is concentrated in the south and around a few northern cities.

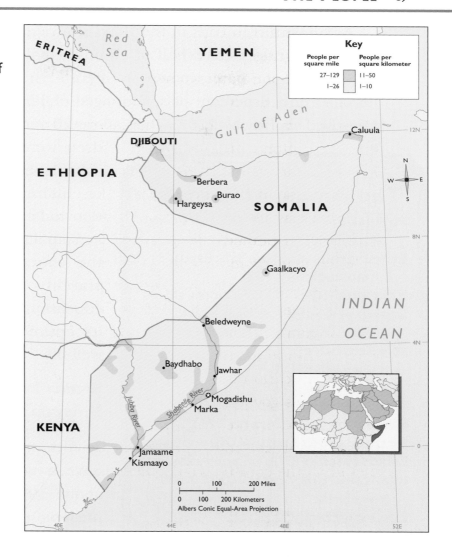

Many religious schools have also opened. The Islamic group Al Islah has put together a network of primary and secondary schools in locations throughout Somalia. Persian Gulf countries and Kenya have supplied curriculum materials; funding has come from Kuwait, Saudi Arabia, and the United Arab Emirates. Other Islamic groups have also established schools. While Al Islah favors a progressive version of Islam, some fundamentalist Islamic schools segregate boys and girls and require girls to wear head-scarves, according to Islamic tradition.

Among the countries in the Horn of Africa, Somalia has the lowest literacy rate. About half of all adult males can read, but only one-quarter of Somali women are literate. In 1996 primary schools enrolled only 8 percent of school-aged children. That number had improved slightly by 2007, when about 20 percent of Somalia's children were enrolled in primary schools. But the small numbers of children receiving an education indicate that literacy rates in Somalia will remain low until the country achieves political stability and establishes an educational system that serves its entire people, not just the well-off.

SOMALI POETRY AND STORYTELLING

Although Somalis did not have a written language until about 1972, they managed to preserve their legends and history through the country's strong oral traditions. For hundreds of years, Somalis have memorized stories and poems word-for-word, passing them down from one generation to the next. Many present-day Somalis can recite poems that are centuries old, and credit the original author as well.

The People of Somalia

Population: 9,832,017* (3.5 million in Somaliland)

Ethnic groups: Somali, 85%; Bantu, Arab, and other, 15%

Religions: Sunni Muslim (almost all)

Languages: Somali (official), Arabic, Italian, English

Age structure:
0–14 years: 45%
15–64 years: 52.6%
65 years and over: 2.5%

Population growth rate: 2.815%

Birth rate: 44.12 births/1,000 population

Death rate: 15.89/1,000 population

Infant mortality rate: 109.19/1,000 live births

Life expectancy at birth:
total population: 49.63 years
males: 47.78 years
females: 51.53 years

Total fertility rate: 6.52 children born/woman

Literacy: 37.8 percent (2001 est.)

*The population count is difficult to determine because of nomad and refugee movement due to famine and clan warfare.
All figures are 2009 estimates unless otherwise indicated.
Source: CIA World Factbook, 2009.

Verbal ability, especially with poetry, is highly valued in Somali society. In fact, poetry and Islam have been described as the twin pillars of Somali culture. In this country, men skilled in poetry command great prestige and even political power.

Poetry topics cover all aspects of life—love, death, religious faith, current events, politics and government, even praises for the hardy camel. Somalis compete among themselves at poetry contests, in which they must compose and recite poetry on the spot.

Another oral tradition in Somalia is storytelling. Unlike poetry contests, storytelling takes place among family and friends, often while sitting outdoors in the evening. Older family members usually take turns reciting clan history, telling religious stories, or relating tales that have been handed down for generations.

CUSTOMS

Somalis live according to the laws and traditions of Islam, which dictate how Muslims should eat, dress, and raise their families. Muslim men and women are separated in most aspects of life.

In Islamic culture, daily tasks are performed using the right hand, which is considered clean, or *xalaal*. Somalis usually eat using the first three fingers of the right hand. The right hand is also used for daily tasks such as writing or shaking hands (men shake hands only with other men, and women only with other women; according to Islamic custom, men and women are not supposed to touch one another unless they are married).

The Muslim diet should consist of *halal* foods (*halal* is Arabic for "allowable," as opposed to *haram*, which means "forbidden"). According to *Sharia*, Muslims may not eat pork or lard, drink alcohol, or smoke cigarettes. Although some urban Somalis may use tobacco or drink alcohol, most refuse to eat pork. The meat that Somalis do eat must be slaughtered in a specific way, while prayers are recited, so that it is *xalaal*.

FOOD

Because of their extreme poverty, many Somali nomads live with hunger. The main diet of pastoral nomads consists of goat and camel milk, *ghee* (liquid butter), and meat. Camel milk is preferred, as it is considered more nutritious than goat milk. **Otka**, dried camel meat that has been fried in butter and spices, provides nourishment during long journeys. However, nomads usually consider their animals too valuable to kill and eat, preferring to trade them for other goods, such as rice, corn, sorghum, tea, sugar, or condiments. When food grains are available, they are used to make bread or porridge. Meals may also be supplemented with roots, wild berries, and other fruits found growing in the wild.

The farmers in southern Somalia eat the same foods as the northern nomads, but their diet usually includes more cereal grains, legumes, vegetables, and fruits (bananas, citrus fruits, mangoes, and papayas). They make porridge, called **soor**, from sorghum, and **anjeero**, a flat bread that looks like a pancake.

Before the war, urban residents could often choose from an even larger variety of foods. City marketplaces offered not only foods grown in Somalia, but also imported foods such as spaghetti (known as *baasto*), canned goods, rice, coffee, and black or brown teas. Because of Somalia's political instability and lack of security, however, imports are sporadic and food shortages are common.

A favorite Somali meal is pasta with marinara sauce, a habit developed during Italy's occupation of the south. Other typical Somali foods include *muufo*, a flat bread made of oats or corn; *sambusas*, which are deep-fried, triangular-shaped dumplings filled with meat or vegetables; porridge made of millet or cornmeal; or rice or noodles with sauce. Beverages might include black tea sweetened with milk and sugar, or juices from mangos and guavas, which come from farm plantations located in the Jubba River

A Somali man prepares to bake bread in an outdoor oven in the Lugh Ganane desert, west of Mogadishu. *Anjeero*, a flat bread that resembles a pancake, is particularly popular in southern Somalia.

Basin. The midday meal is the main meal of the day.

Rural Somalis cook food outdoors, usually over a charcoal fire. In the cities, wealthier Somalis can prepare foods in well-equipped kitchens, in some cases with modern appliances such as toasters and microwaves, supplied by family members or other relatives living and working abroad.

CLOTHING

Somali men and women often wear Western-style clothing, especially at work or school. But during leisure time and in rural areas, many people prefer the traditional Somali dress, as the clothing is loose and comfortable.

According to Islamic tradition, men should wear clothes that cover the body from the waist to the knees. Somali men may wear the *futa* (also called *maro* or *tob*), which consists of several lengths of white cotton wrapped around the waist like a kilt, then draped over the shoulder. Or they may wear a **macaawiis**, a brightly colored cloth similar to an Indonesian sarong. Some Somali men wear a snug-fitting cap, called a *benadiry kufia*.

The traditional dress for Somali women is the *hijab*, a colorful, full-length dress that covers the entire body except for the hands and face. The traditional Somali *guntiino* is similar to an Indian sari, but usually consists of plain white or red cotton.

According to Islamic tradition, married women are expected to cover their body from head to toe, although most Somali women do not cover their faces but simply cover their hair with colorful head-scarves. However, women of fundamentalist Islamic sects wear a *niqab*, a veil that covers part of the face. In the past, single women braided their hair and did not wear perfume or incense until they were married. However, this tradition is not always followed today.

In Somalia, people make use of cosmetics derived from plants. To condition hair and give it a rich chestnut color, both men and women apply a plant-based dye called **henna**. Men may also use it on their beard to tone down the gray. Women also use henna, and another plant-based dye called *khidaab*, to apply elaborately styl-ized decorations to the foot up to the ankle, or the hand up to the wrist. These intricate designs are usually worn when celebrating joyous occasions, such as marriage or the birth of a baby.

MARRIAGE AND FAMILY

In the past, most marriages were arranged. That is, parents of a prospective bride and groom would decide upon a suitable match

On special occasions such as weddings, Somali women use plant-based dyes to adorn their hands with elaborate designs.

and make plans for them to wed. Marriages between two people of different clans helped ensure that clan alliances remained strong. Today fewer arranged marriages take place, as more couples are marrying for love, although parents might still try to prevent a match they consider unsuitable. The average age of a Somali bride is 14 or 15.

According to Islamic tradition, men may marry up to four wives at one time, although only about one-fifth of Somali husbands have more than one wife. In urban areas the husband provides separate residences for his different families. However, in rural areas there is usually a single household, and the wives and children care for the farm or livestock together. Divorce is allowed under Islamic law, but the husband is the only one who can initiate the process.

Somalis may also live with extended family, such as grandparents and married sons and their families. Young adults who move to the city to go to school or work generally stay with relatives, rather than live alone.

The average Somali woman has seven children; the more children she bears, the greater her status in her culture. Births occur at home and are attended by a midwife.

HOUSING AND HANDICRAFTS

Pastoral nomads use a movable hut called an **aqal**, in which they may sleep, shelter their babies, or store fresh milk. Usually built by women, the *aqal* consists of long green branches that have been bent into the shape of an arch, then tied together with ropes to form a domed structure about 6 feet (1.8 meters) in diameter. A center pole supports the roof, which, like the walls, is covered with animal hides or with mats woven from grass. The finished dwelling can be easily dismantled when it is time to move to new pasturelands. Nomads tie the sticks and grass mats onto a camel, making room for babies and small children to ride on top.

Because the nomadic life requires frequent moves, household items are few and light. The typical family may carry leather water bags, wooden jugs and mats, stools, camel bells, spoons, and food supplies, using containers that can be easily tied onto the camel.

Farmers who have settled in one location usually build a one-room structure called a *mundul.* Like the *aqal*, it has a circular framework of poles and a central supporting pole, but the outside is plastered with mud and covered by a thatched or metal roof. Owners furnish these rural dwellings with rough wooden furniture and pottery.

In small towns or on the outskirts of cities, Somalis may build a version of the *aqal* that is covered with cardboard or cloth, instead of skins and grasses. A more permanent building found in cities is the *arish*, a rectangular structure often made of mud walls, with a tin or thatched roof. The *sar* is a building made of cement or concrete. Before the civil war, cities contained a range of architecture that varied from Arab-style houses to Italian villas, with many buildings constructed of sturdy concrete, stone, or bricks. Few Somali homes had screened or glass-covered openings, although the homes of wealthy merchants featured beautiful doors, carved by local carpenters. Years of gun battles, bombings, and looting have reduced many of these architectural treasures to rubble.

For nomads, the arts must be practical. Women, in particular, become skilled at using materials in the world around them to fashion items that serve a useful purpose. From grasses, they weave mats and baskets, as well as containers that are woven so tightly they can hold water or milk. Using timber, men or women may carve wooden spoons, drinking cups, milk jugs, headrests, or containers to hold cosmetics, medications, powders, or other small items. Wooden milk jugs are often embellished with decorative carved patterns.

HEALTH

Years of floods and droughts, warfare, extreme poverty, inadequate nutrition, and insufficient medical care have combined to give Somalia the highest infant mortality rate and the second-lowest life expectancy (next to Djibouti) of all the nations in the Horn of Africa. For every 1,000 Somali babies born, more than 105 will die before their first birthday; overall life expectancy for Somalis is only about 49 years.

With no central government (and, in many cases, no municipal government) to provide, oversee, or maintain health and sanitation facilities, disease is rampant in Somalia. The main causes of death by disease are diarrhea, acute respiratory infections (such as pneumonia), measles, malaria, and tetanus. Other major diseases include tuberculosis and parasitic and venereal infections.

People living near Somalia's two major rivers are particularly vulnerable to malaria, a tropical disease carried by mosquitoes. Besides disease-bearing mosquitoes, the marshy areas along the rivers also harbor snails that carry a parasitic worm that causes schistosomiasis, a disabling intestinal illness. Young children are particularly susceptible to such parasitic infections, which can be fatal. Tuberculosis is most prevalent among young male nomads,

The *aqal*, a portable hut consisting of a frame of bent green branches that is covered with animal hides or woven grass mats, serves as shelter for Somalia's nomads. By tradition, women are usually responsible for constructing the *aqal*.

who spread the disease as they travel from place to place. Contaminated water has been the cause of annual outbreaks of cholera.

Medical care in Somalia is minimal. According to U.N. figures, there are only 0.4 doctors and 2 nurses available to treat every 100,000 Somalis. Just 1.5 percent of children between one and two years old have received all necessary vaccinations. As a result, one out of every four Somali children dies before reaching the age of five.

> **Due to sustained drought conditions, in early 2003 less than 20 percent of the population in central and southern Somalia had access to safe drinking water.**

In Somalia, girls as well as boys are circumcised, usually between birth and age five. Circumcision is viewed as a necessary rite of passage to adulthood and as the way for both men and women to be *xalaal*, or pure. In Somalia, boys are usually circumcised during a religious ritual that includes prayers and the slaying of a goat.

The circumcision of girls is common in several countries of the Middle East and Africa, including Somalia. Many Somali girls and women suffer from health problems as a result of the procedure. Some even die from blood loss, tetanus, or other infections. Nevertheless, 98 percent of Somali women are circumcised. If they were not, they would be considered unclean according to their culture—and unmarriageable.

Fighting and famine have displaced hundreds of thousands of Somalis. Here a woman stands outside her tent at a refugee camp in the Woqooyi Galbeed region of Somalia.

Communities

Somalia is officially divided into 18 administrative regions, or *gobolka*. Although the federal government does not have much authority over these provinces today, each has a capital city and most have some kind of local governing body. In some cases, the *gobolka* is divided among numerous military factions (for example, Benadir, which contains the city of Mogadishu). In other cases, several *gobolka* have been combined under the rule of a single government (for example, Somaliland, Puntland, or the State of Southwestern Somalia).

Although most of its people lived in rural areas before the civil war, Somalia has seen a major shift in population as fighting has driven nomads and farmers to urban areas. During the 1990s, regional droughts and floods also displaced many citizens, who flocked to city refugee camps in search of food and medical help. At the same time, as bandits and warring factions took control of sections of the cities, many residents fled the country to refugee camps outside of Somalia.

Most of Somalia's important cities and towns are located along the coast and were established more than 1,000 years ago, during Arab rule. The four major ports are Mogadishu, Berbera, Kismaayo, and Marka. The largest inland city, Hargeysa, also owes its growth to trade, mostly in livestock.

MOGADISHU

Located about 140 miles (225 km) north of the equator, on the southeastern coast of Somalia, the port city of Mogadishu (also spelled Muqdisho) is Somalia's capital and its largest city. Once home to over than a million people, the city has suffered severe damage since the battles in 1991 between President Siad Barre's army and anti-government forces. The anarchy that followed has allowed for little rebuilding, as the Transitional Federal Government and armed political factions continue to fight over control of the capital.

The trading center of Mogadishu was founded in the ninth century by Arab and Persian traders, who named it "the seat of the Shah." Arab sultans ruled the city for several centuries. In 1871 Mogadishu came under the control of the sultan of Zanzibar, who built the Garesa Palace, a notable landmark that later housed the Somali National Museum. During the 20th century the city served as the capital of Italian Somaliland, the Somali Republic, and the Somali Democratic Republic. Today Mogadishu serves as the base of the Transitional Federal Government.

Before the civil war, Mogadishu was Somalia's principal port of entry, a modern deepwater port that handled most of the country's exports, including bananas, cattle, and hides. It was also the leading commercial and manufacturing center, with industries that processed foods (meat and fish), leather, wood products, and textiles.

Closed during the war, the port is now open, but pirates often ambush ships. The city's international airport closed in 1995.

The city's central section once contained Mediterranean-style architecture, reflecting the influence of more than half a century of Italian occupation. However, warfare destroyed most of its landmarks, including a Roman Catholic cathedral (one of the few Christian places of worship to be found in Muslim-dominated Somalia) and the Garesa Palace.

Still, many entrepreneurs have reopened old businesses or started up new ones in Mogadishu. Its central marketplace, called Bakara, offers a variety of goods. Although most of the city's schools, including the Somali National University, closed because of the war, well-to-do Somalis can send their children to Benadir University, which opened in 1991.

HARGEYSA

Located in Somalia's interior, in the Ogo highlands, the city of Hargeysa (also spelled Hargeisa) has a population of more than 240,000, which makes it Somalia's second-largest city. Although not officially recognized as an independent nation, the Republic of Somaliland has based its government in Hargeysa, making the city its capital. Hargeysa had served as a capital city once before, from 1941 to 1960, when the area was a British protectorate.

Extensive bombing in May 1988 by Siad Barre's government forces virtually destroyed Hargeysa, but, despite occasional sectarian violence, the city has been rebuilding since Somaliland proclaimed its independence in 1991. For many years Hargeysa has been a center for Somalia's trade in livestock, as well as wool, hides, and skins. Its surrounding area receives enough rainfall to support the farming of corn and sorghum.

As the government of Somaliland continues to benefit from foreign aid and loans, efforts to rebuild the city should progress more rapidly. Hargeysa has Somalia's only traffic lights. The city is home to the University of Hargeysa, founded in 1998, and to an airport that serves various airlines.

BERBERA

Boasting Somalia's only sheltered harbor, Berbera serves as the major port of Somaliland. Somalia's third-largest city, with a population of about 220,000, it is situated on the northwestern coast. Berbera receives general cargo for the northern part of the country and handles much of the nation's livestock exports. Other exports include gum arabic (made from the sap of acacia trees), frankincense, and myrrh. Much of this trade is with Aden, which is located across the Red Sea, in Yemen.

Berbera, located along the northwestern coast, is a major port. With more than 200,000 residents, it is also Somalia's third-largest city.

Historical records indicate that Berbera was operating as a trade center by the 1200s. For a short time in the late 1800s, it was controlled by Egypt. Subsequently, the British took over, and Berbera was the capital of British Somaliland until 1941.

In 1969 the Soviet Union provided funding to modernize Berbera's deepwater port in exchange for the right to maintain a naval and missile base there. The United States, which took over the former Soviet base in the late 1970s, spent $37 million on improvements to the harbor in 1985. But since then the facilities have become run-down. Berbera also has a small airport.

KISMAAYO

Kismaayo (also spelled Kismayu, Chisimaio, and Kismaio) is located in southern Somalia, just south of where the Jubba River enters the Indian Ocean. With its deepwater port, this city of around 210,000 has served as an export center for Somalia-raised bananas and meat. As a principal commercial and manufacturing center, Kismaayo once housed industries that processed meat, fish, turtle, and leather. Ongoing factional fighting has disrupted much of this industry, however.

Kismaayo was founded as a trading center in 1872 by the sultan of Zanzibar, who also built a palace and several mosques there. The British occupied the town in 1887, and from 1927 to 1941 it was part of Italian Somaliland. The United States financed the $42 million renovation of Kismaayo's deepwater port in the latter half of the 1980s. A small, local airstrip serves the city, which is also home to about 15,000 internally displaced Somalis.

MARKA

The city of Marka is a lighterage port, which means that the loading and unloading of ships takes place while the vessels are anchored offshore. Located in southeastern Somalia, just south of

Mogadishu, this city—which is also spelled Merka or Merca—has a population of about 180,000. It is an export point for bananas, and it hosts several industries, including oilseed processing, fishing, and the manufacture of textiles, boats, and paper products.

Life and death in Baidoa: While a group of men lounge in the shade of a building, a victim of starvation lies nearby. This gruesome scene was photographed in August 1992, at the beginning of a pitiless famine that claimed the lives of 40 percent of Baidoa's residents in a four-month period.

BAIDOA

Located in southwestern Somalia, the inland city of Baidoa (or Baydhabo)—population about 80,000—is the capital of the Bay region, one of the two main areas in Somalia where cereal grain is cultivated. Baidoa has served as a major marketplace and a hub from which food was trucked to Somalian ports.

But the town suffered from a severe famine that killed at least 40 percent of the population between the months of August and November 1992, according to a study by the U.S. Centers for Disease Control. To prevent further deaths, which at the time averaged more than 300 per day, the United Nations helped institute a massive feeding and medical program for the people of Baidoa. Although the influx of food and medical assistance reduced the number of deaths, ongoing clan violence between warlords continued to take a steep toll.

In 1998 the major clan of the area, the Rahanwayn, and its armed political faction, the Rahanwayn Resistance Army, captured Baidoa from forces loyal to Hussein Mohammad Aidid. In 2002, rival factions within the RRA began to fight for control of the city. The resulting battles killed hundreds and displaced thousands more. The Islamist militia al-Shabaab seized control of Baidoa and imposed *Sharia* in early 2009.

BOSSASO

By 1997 the port of Bossaso, located on the northeastern coast of Somalia, had become a major point of entry for foreign goods. Today the town, which has a population of around 33,000 and is also called Bender Cassim, is the largest city in Puntland, the breakaway nation that came into existence in 1998. Although Bossaso does not serve as Puntland's official capital, the thriving port city is its commercial center. Trade-related businesses in the city have continued to flourish despite recent disputes over Puntland's leadership.

Bossaso contains Puntland's only institution of higher learning, the East Africa University, which opened its doors in 2000. East Africa University offers courses of study at its College of Sharia and Islamic Studies, and at its College of Business Administration.

Factional disputes within Somalia have contributed to the growth of Bossaso's population. About 28,000 internally displaced persons live in five refugee camps located on the outskirts of the city. Many fled fighting in the Jubba and Shabeelle River regions of southern Somalia in 1993.

HOLIDAYS AND CELEBRATIONS

Somalis celebrate public holidays such as New Year's on January 1 and Labor Day on May 1. They also commemorate political holidays. People in northern Somalia observe Independence Day on June 26, the anniversary of the date British Somaliland became independent. All Somalis mark National Day on July 1, the date that Italian Somaliland achieved independence and then united with the former British protectorate to create the Somali Republic in 1960.

But of far more importance to Somalia's overwhelmingly Muslim population are the major Islamic holidays. The Islamic calendar, which is based on lunar months (each month begins when the crescent moon first becomes visible after a new moon), determines when these holidays are celebrated. Because the Islamic year is slightly longer than 354 days, Muslim holidays shift back about 11 days each year with respect to the Western calendar.

The five pillars of Islam require that Muslims observe Ramadan, a period of prayer and fasting that occurs during the ninth month of the Islamic calendar. During the 30 days of Ramadan, adults pray, fast, and refrain from drinking during the daylight hours;

they eat only in the evening. (Children under 15 are usually exempt from these restrictions.)

The holiday of Eid al-Fitr (the Feast of Breaking the Fast) marks the end of Ramadan. During this time, family members dress in their best clothes and come together with friends and relatives for

Muslims on the hajj, the annual pilgrimage to Mecca, pray before the Ka'aba. The shrine is said to have been built by the patriarch Ibrahim (Abraham).

> **Somali names have three parts: the individual's given name, the father's name, and the paternal grandfather's name. Brothers and sisters of the same parents share the same second and third names. However, their mother remains affiliated with her clan of birth and does not change her name when she marries.**

feasts, prayers, and the exchange of gifts. Eid al-Fitr celebrations often last for up to three days.

The 12th month of the Islamic calendar is the time of the hajj, the pilgrimage to Mecca, in Saudi Arabia. According to the five pillars of Islam, all Muslims who are able to make the hajj are supposed to do so once in their lifetime. The hajj culminates on the 10th day of the month with the most important Muslim holiday, Eid al-Adha, or the Feast of Sacrifice.

Eid al-Adha honors the devotion to Allah of the Muslim patriarch Ibrahim, who was prepared to sacrifice his son as commanded. At the last moment Allah provided a ram for sacrifice instead. Somali Muslims commemorate the holiday with special prayers and the ritual sacrifice of a goat or sheep. They set aside a portion of the meat for the poor and share the rest with family and friends. Three days of feasting and celebration follow, as friends visit each other's homes, children receive presents, and families visit the graves of their ancestors.

Muslims mark the Islamic New Year with a 10-day celebration, beginning on the first day of Muharram (the first month of the Islamic calendar). On the 10th day of Muharram, Muslims celebrate Ashura, which marks the murder, in 680, of Hussein, a grandson of Muhammad. The observance of Ashura serves to remind Muslims of the sacrifices made by the Prophet's family.

Muslims honor Muhammad on Mouloud (Maulid An-Nabi), or

the Birth of the Prophet, which falls on the 12th day of the third month of the Islamic calendar. Although the holiday is actually the anniversary of the Prophet's death, it serves as a day of remembrance. Devout Muslims spend the day praying, reading the Qur'an, and telling stories and poems honoring Muhammad.

Somali festivities also take place during family events, such as the naming of a newborn, the circumcision of boys, and engagement and marriage celebrations. All involve large family gatherings and plenty of food. Like many religious holidays, the naming and circumcision ceremonies are also accompanied by prayers and the ritual killing of a goat. Marriage celebrations often feature seven consecutive days of dancing.

A U.S. Black Hawk helicopter circles the darkening skies of Mogadishu, September 1993. Originally deployed to Somalia as part of a United Nations humanitarian mission called Operation Restore Hope, American troops were eventually drawn into fighting with a clan-based faction.

Foreign Relations

After Somalia became an independent nation in 1960, its government attempted to diversify and modernize the economy through a series of development plans, mostly funded by foreign grants and loans. During the 1960s, the Somalian government accepted aid from Western nations such as the United States, Italy, and the Federal Republic of Germany, as well as from communist-ruled countries such as the Soviet Union and China.

When Mohamed Siad Barre assumed power in 1969, he aligned Somalia with the Soviet Union, which funneled aid to the African country throughout much of the 1970s. At the same time, Siad Barre's government also reached out to Arab countries. In 1974 Somalia became the only non-Arabic-speaking member of the Arab League, an organization designed to promote the common interests of Arab states.

When the Soviet Union sided with Ethiopia during the

1977–78 Ogaden War, Somalia severed relations with the Soviets and turned to the United States and Western Europe for economic and military assistance. At the time, the United States was locked in a struggle for global political supremacy with the Soviet Union. That struggle, which emerged in the wake of World War II, was known as the cold war. Within Europe, the lines were clearly drawn: the United States counted among its allies the democratic nations of Western Europe; the Soviet Union dominated the communist countries of Eastern Europe. Elsewhere, however, potential allies of the two superpowers—and thus a strategic advantage—were often up for grabs.

So when the Soviet Union forged a close relationship with Ethiopia in 1977, thereby increasing its influence in the strategic

Fighters of the Western Somalia Liberation Front, in the Ogaden region of Ethiopia. In 1977 and 1978, Somalia and Ethiopia fought a war over control of the Ogaden, which is home to many ethnic Somalis.

Horn of Africa, the United States and its allies were alarmed. Thus they were willing to pour money into Somalia to counterbalance the Soviet gains. In return for U.S. economic development aid and military support, Somalia gave the United States access to ports and airfields in Berbera, Mogadishu, and Kismaayo. But in 1989, as the cold war was winding down, the United States withdrew its support for Siad Barre's government because of its poor human rights record.

NEED FOR INTERNATIONAL ASSISTANCE

In the decade following the collapse of Siad Barre's regime, the governments of several countries—including Ethiopia, Egypt, Yemen, Kenya, and Italy—attempted to mediate Somalia's internal disputes by bringing the warring factions together for peace talks. But it was not until 2000, at the Djibouti peace conference, that significant progress was made. The United Nations and other intergovernmental organizations, including the European Union and the Arab League, supported the 2000 reconciliation talks that established Somalia's Transitional National Government. And several countries and organizations recognized its legitimacy by sending representatives to the August 27 inauguration ceremony of its president, Abdulkassim Salat Hassan.

The TFG has established diplomatic relations with several countries and has ambassadors in Djibouti and Saudi Arabia. The interim government represents Somalia in the United Nations, the African Union (formerly the Organization of African Unity), and the Arab League. Somalia is also a member of the Common Market for Eastern and Southern Africa (COMESA) and the Intergovernmental Authority on Development (IGAD).

Although international organizations officially recognize the TFG, relatively little monetary aid has been distributed. Some Western nations have withheld funding until the TFG proves its effectiveness. Prominent officials overseeing international efforts in Somalia—including Osman Ali Ahmed, head of the U.N. relief office in Mogadishu—have been assassinated. The lack of reliable economic statistics, Somalia's huge foreign debt, and the country's ongoing political instability and violence have prevented the World Bank from making significant loans to the fledgling government.

The TFG is caught in the middle: without funds to pay law enforcement and military forces, it remains weak, unable to control territory beyond a small sector of Mogadishu. Armed opposition from regional warlords and the Islamist insurgency further hinders any progress the new government hopes to make.

SOMALIA AND ITS NEIGHBORING STATES

A number of people in Somalia support pan-Somalism, the belief that the country should be united with all the surrounding regions that contain ethnic Somalis. This principle pertains directly to Somalia's neighbors Djibouti, Kenya, and Ethiopia, all of which contain regions with majority Somali populations. More than 280,000 ethnic Somalis live in Djibouti; Ethiopia's eastern region and Kenya's northern frontier contain another 3 million people of Somali ancestry.

The tiny country of Djibouti, located northwest of Somalia, gained independence from France in 1977. At the time, it rejected the idea of merging with Siad Barre's Somali Democratic Republic, and since then Djibouti has become firmly established as an independent state. But Djibouti and Somalia have a close bond, as their people share a common culture and language.

The Djibouti government has established economic ties and border agreements with the government of the Republic of Somaliland, which borders the small nation. No visa is required for travel between the two countries. However, Djibouti politically supports Somalia's Transitional Federal Government in Mogadishu, which bitterly opposes the existence of the independent Republic of Somaliland.

Unlike Djibouti, Ethiopia has had a long history of conflict with Somalia, mostly over the Somalian claim to the Ogaden, located in eastern Ethiopia. After World War II, the United Kingdom ceded to Ethiopia the Ogaden, which was inhabited by an ethnic Somali majority. Over the years the Somalian and Ethiopian governments have contested rights to the region, with border conflicts escalating

A Somali mother and child at the Liboi refugee camp in Kenya. Although the economic and political situation in Somalia has not markedly improved, Kenya and Ethiopia have repatriated tens of thousands of Somali refugees.

into open warfare in 1964 and 1977. Most of the southern half of Somalia's western boundary with Ethiopia remains in dispute, although in 1994 Ethiopia hoped to appease its own ethnic Somali citizens by approving a national constitution that provided for a separate Somali state within the country.

Historically, Ethiopia, with its large Christian population, has also been at odds with Muslim-dominated Somalia for religious reasons. In the mid-1990s, concerned that the Islamist militant group Al-Ittihad Al-Islami planned to make Somalia an Islamic state, Ethiopia sent troops into Somalia. The forces joined the Somali Salvation Democratic Front to drive out Al-Ittihad. (The SSDF later established the breakaway region of Puntland.) For a time, Ethiopia sheltered warlord Hussein Mohammad Aidid and backed the Rahanwayn Resistance Army.

With U.N. approval, Ethiopia sent troops into Baidoa in July 2006 to aid the Somali TFG in its bloody fight against the Islamic Courts Union. By January 2007, TFG forces had regained control of most areas, but insurgents refused to attend Ethiopia-backed peace talks. Many Somalis, including non-ICU supporters, viewed the Ethiopians as invaders. Ethiopian troops officially withdrew in early 2009, as promised by the TFG, but allegedly kept a covert presence.

Kenya's northern border has seen a number of clashes as well. Shortly after gaining independence in 1960, the Republic of Somalia severed diplomatic ties with the United Kingdom because of a dispute over ownership of the northeastern region of Kenya. Although the majority population of Kenya's Northern Frontier District is ethnic Somali, Siad Barre relinquished his claim to the region in 1981.

However, disagreements over the territory continued—in 1989 thousands of Somalis were expelled from areas near Kenya's game preserves because of accusations they had been poaching elephants. The lack of border security between the two countries gave rise to growing concerns that militants based in Somalia were crossing into Kenya to commit terrorist attacks.

During the late 1980s and the 1990s, Somalia's neighbors took in hundreds of thousands of refugees, who were given housing in refugee camps located along the borders of Ethiopia and Kenya. Despite the continuing violence in Somalia, in the mid-1990s these nations began to repatriate (send back to their home country) the Somali refugees. In 2001 the Kenyan government ordered 15,000 Somali refugees to return home. And of the eight camps established in Ethiopia, six had been shut down by the fall of 2002.

Djibouti, Ethiopia, and Kenya are all members of the Intergovernmental Authority on Development (IGAD), sponsor of Somali peace talks begun in 2002 and funded by the European Union and the United States. Djibouti hosted the initial conference, and Kenya became host of the follow-up reconciliation talks. In 2007, the U.N. authorized an African Union peacekeeping mission in Somalia, a plan that included troop deployments.

SOMALIA AND THE EUROPEAN UNION

First established in 1993, the European Union (EU) consists of countries from the continent of Europe that work together politically and economically. The 12 original members of the EU previously belonged to the European Community, which included two countries with ties to Somalia—Great Britain and Italy.

After Somalia gained independence in 1960, the European Community played a major role in funding projects to aid in the country's economic development. Since 1995 the European Union has been the largest donor to Somalia and has played a key role in shaping international policies toward the country.

Much of the EU's funding has gone to Somaliland, which has managed to maintain a stable government in the midst of Somalia's anarchy. In 2003 the European Commission (the EU's executive body) approved funds and technical assistance for infrastructure improvements within the Republic of Somaliland, including the repair of major roads, rehabilitation of the port in Berbera, and reestablishment of urban water supply systems.

In early 2003, the European Commission approved a 5-million-euro (about $5 million) humanitarian aid package that would benefit people struggling for survival in central and southern Somalia. This program specifically targeted the problem areas of health, water, sanitation, and food security.

SOMALIA, THE UNITED STATES, AND THE WAR ON TERRORISM

The 1993 Battle of Mogadishu—during which 18 U.S. servicemen lost their lives in support of United Nations peacekeeping efforts—dampened the enthusiasm of American policymakers for humanitarian missions in places such as Somalia, where the United States had no vital strategic interests at stake. Within a decade, however, terrorism would reorient the thinking of American officials. On September 11, 2001, supporters of the Islamic fundamentalist group al-Qaeda flew two hijacked jetliners into the World Trade Center in New York City and one into the Pentagon in Washington, D.C. A fourth hijacked plane, believed to be headed for the White House or the U.S. Capitol, crashed in a field in western Pennsylvania after passengers attempted to overpower the hijackers. More than 3,000 people died in the terrorist attacks, which stunned the nation.

Al-Qaeda, founded around 1989 by a wealthy Saudi named Osama bin Laden, was dedicated to opposing non-Islamic governments with violence. Bin Laden was particularly fervent about driving U.S. armed forces out of the Arabian Peninsula and the Horn of Africa, including Somalia.

In the investigations that followed the September 11 attacks, the U.S. government became concerned that Osama bin Laden and his followers had been using Somalia as a base for their terrorist operations. There was speculation that bin Laden had sent several top lieutenants to Somalia in the early 1990s to provide assistance to Mohammad Farrah Aidid, the local warlord who had violently resisted the U.N. peacekeeping efforts in 1993. Some analysts believed that after U.S. troops withdrew in 1994, al-Qaeda supporters had remained in the country.

U.S. intelligence reports indicated that Somalia contained numerous terrorist training camps that belonged to the Islamic

Rescue workers search for buried victims after a car-bomb attack on the U.S. embassy in Nairobi, Kenya, August 7, 1998. The attack—and another on the same day against the U.S. embassy in Dar es Salaam, Tanzania—was linked to Al-Ittihad Al-Islami, a Somalian group with ties to the al-Qaeda terrorist organization. U.S. analysts and policymakers worry that continued chaos could make Somalia a haven for Islamic terrorists.

fundamentalist group Al-Ittihad Al-Islami. Bin Laden had visited these camps in the mid-1990s, but they were abandoned. It appeared that after being defeated in central and northeast Somalia by the Somali Salvation Democratic Front and Ethiopian troops, Al-Ittihad had gone underground. Still, Al-Ittihad terrorists were linked to the deadly 1998 bombings of the U.S. embassies in Dar es Salaam, Tanzania, and in Nairobi, Kenya.

In the weeks following the September 11 terrorist attacks, President George W. Bush targeted Somalia for its connections to bin Laden. In November the Bush administration froze financial assets of al-Barakaat, Somalia's largest *hawala*, because of alleged links to al-Qaeda terrorists. Besides money transfer services, al-Barakaat operated telecommunications services and soft drink industries; it was the biggest employer in Somalia, and its closure cost hundreds of Somalis their jobs.

Of even greater impact was the loss of money normally sent to Somalia through al-Barakaat from Somalis living and working abroad. The flow of remittance funds, Somalia's largest single source of income, was cut in half. Coming at the same time as other economic problems, including severe inflation, drought, and an export ban on livestock, the closure of al-Barakaat devastated the country's economy.

During the cold war, Somalia received more aid per person than any other African nation, first from the Soviet Union and then from the United States.

Besides shutting down al-Barakaat, President Bush also released a list of terrorist organizations, which included the notorious Al-Ittihad Al-Islami, and he ordered stepped-up military activities in and around Somalia. Warships from Britain, Germany, and the United States began patrolling the Somalian coastline to guard against infiltration by terrorists, while American surveillance planes circled overhead, keeping watch for any activity in the vacated training camps. Somalia was even mentioned as a possible target of U.S. attacks, fanning its citizens' fears.

On November 28, 2002, two missiles were fired at an Israeli-chartered jet minutes after it took off from Mombasa airport in Kenya. Around the same time, suicide bombers at an Israeli-owned hotel in the city killed 16 and injured dozens more. Somalia was identified as the most likely source of the missiles and the probable entry point of the suicide bombers. U.S. intelligence officials theorized that the November 28 attacks were the work of an al-Qaeda–al-Ittihad partnership.

Coincidentally, the Pentagon opened an anti-terrorism base in Djibouti around the same time the attacks in Kenya took place. About 1,000 troops, mostly American and German, were given the task of monitoring Somalia, Sudan, and Yemen for possible terrorist activity.

In December 2002, reports of increased activity by local Islamic groups linked to al-Qaeda led to a meeting between U.S. military officials, Somalian political leaders and militia commanders, and Ethiopian leaders. At that time, Somali Restoration and Reconciliation Council head Hussein Mohammad Aidid accused the Transitional National Government of being controlled by Islamic terrorists. The accusation, seen as an attempt to discredit the new government, was not taken seriously. Eventually, the United States turned its attention to Afghanistan, where bin Laden was based.

The United States then took a diplomatic approach to Somalia, funding the 2002 peace talks and pledging support for the TFG, but resumed military activity after the rise of the Islamic Courts Union. U.S. intelligence reports linked the ICU, and subsequently al-Shabaab and other insurgent groups, to al-Qaeda. On at least five occasions in 2007 and 2008, U.S. aircrafts bombed southern Somalia, targeting al-Shabaab and suspected al-Qaeda bases. Some reports of civilian casualties followed the strikes. U.S. Navy ships began to patrol Somali waters in 2008, monitoring pirate activity.

The United States has not had an embassy in Somalia since May 1991. Likewise, there is no Somalian embassy in the United States, though the Transitional National Government maintains a diplomatic mission in Washington, D.C.

A NIGHTMARE WORLD

For more than a decade Somalis have endured a nightmare world of random violence, kidnapping, banditry, and government-sponsored human rights abuses. In city streets particularly, scores of innocent bystanders have been killed in the seemingly endless battles between rival clan militias.

Kidnapping on land and at sea has become a routine way for Somalis to collect debts or simply to raise cash. When the victim is Somali, elders from the kidnappers' and the victim's clan typically negotiate how much money should change hands, though they never refer to the payment as ransom. When the victim is foreign (such as an aid worker, journalist, or passenger on a hijacked vessel), the kidnappers can set their own ransom. In 2008 alone, pirates hijacked 42 ships and collected an estimated $150 million in ransom. In order to protect their guests from the constant threat of kidnapping, Mogadishu hotels now hire militias (often armed teenagers in pickup trucks) to follow the guests as they ride in hotel taxis. However, even with protection, airstrips, armed vehicles, and hotel rooms containing foreigners have all been stormed.

Anyone traveling Somalia's roads risks encountering armed bandits who may demand money or goods in return for safe passage. Such banditry has slowed—and, in some cases, prevented entirely—the delivery of aid to Somalia's desperately needy. Clan factions that control sections of road typically stop the truck caravans of U.N. agencies, aid organizations, and other humanitarian groups to col-

In the absence of a viable central government, real power in Somalia rests largely with clan warlords, whose heavily armed militias do battle with rivals, extort money from travelers and relief agencies, and commit kidnappings for money. The militia fighters shown here are patrolling the streets of Mogadishu in a "technical," a four-wheel-drive vehicle upon which an antiaircraft or heavy machine gun has been mounted.

lect "tolls"—often a portion of the food and medicine the trucks are carrying, which the clans can then sell.

In addition to the threat of random violence and crime, Somalis face human rights abuses at the hands of government officials. Authorities in both Somaliland and Puntland have arrested people merely for attending peace conferences or peace demonstrations. In late 2000 public outcry forced the president of Somaliland to pardon one man who had been jailed for this "offense." In Puntland, demonstrators supporting peace conferences have been attacked and jailed by police. In March 2003 Puntland authorities ordered several human rights groups to shut down because members attended a peace symposium held in Hargeysa.

Until Somalia's countless factions can put aside their differences and agree to work together, the rights of the country's citizens will continue to be denied, their economic prospects will remain bleak, and peace in this war-torn land will remain elusive.

600s: Arab tribes establish the sultanate of Adel on the Gulf of Aden coast.

800s: Immigrants from Yemen and the Persian Gulf settle along the Somali coast.

900s–1500s: Sultanate of Adel breaks up as tribes disperse throughout the area.

1500s–1800s: Somalis settle in eastern region of Ethiopia.

1870s–90s: The French, Italians, Egyptians, and British occupy parts of Somalia; the three European powers and Ethiopia eventually divide the region.

1899–1920: Mohammed ibn Abdullah Hassan revolts against occupation.

1936: Italy conquers part of Ethiopia, combines Italian Somaliland with Somali-speaking parts to form Italian East Africa.

1940: Italian troops occupy British Somaliland.

1941: British retake British Somaliland and occupy Italian Somaliland.

1949–50: U.N. trust territory of Italian Somaliland is established under Italian control.

1960: British Somaliland and Italian Somaliland gain independence, unite on July 1 to form the Republic of Somalia; Aden Abdullah Osman is elected as the country's first president.

1967: Abdi Rashid Ali Shermarke defeats Osman in presidential elections.

1969: Mohamed Siad Barre assumes power in bloodless military coup after President Shermarke is assassinated.

1970: Siad Barre declares Somalia a socialist state and nationalizes banks, petroleum companies, and other businesses.

1972: Official written script for the Somali language is developed.

1977: Somalia invades Ogaden region of Ethiopia, severs diplomacy with Soviet Union.

1978: Somalia withdraws from Ogaden in March.

1988: Somalia signs nonaggression treaty with Ethiopia; Siad Barre has northern Somalia bombed after Somali National Movement takeover of the region.

1990: Armed uprising erupts in Mogadishu in December.

1991: *January*: Siad Barre flees the country; United Somali Congress (USC) captures Mogadishu. *May*: Somaliland declares independence.

1992: U.N. peacekeeping force, including U.S. Marines, arrives in Somalia.

1993: *May*: Breakaway Somaliland elects Mohammed Ibrahim Egal as president. *June*: Forces of Mogadishu warlord Mohammad Farrah Aidid kill 24 Pakistani peacekeepers. *July*: Somali hostility toward U.N. forces rises when American soldiers kill 50 unarmed Somalis. *October*: Battle in Mogadishu between U.S. troops and Aidid's forces and Somali civilians kills 18 Americans and hundreds of Somalis.

1995: All U.N. peacekeeping troops withdraw; Mohammad Farrah Aidid declares himself president of Somalia.

1996: Aidid dies and is succeeded by his son, Hussein Mohammad Aidid.

1997: Faction leaders meet in Cairo, Egypt, for peace talks but fail to agree.

1998: Puntland region in northeastern Somalia declares independence.

2000: In October, the Transitional National Government (TNG) begins work in Mogadishu.

2001: *May*: Dozens killed in Mogadishu, in battles between TNG and Somali Restoration and Reconciliation Council (SRRC), led by Hussein Aidid. September: U.N. and European Union evacuate foreign aid workers in wake of terrorist attacks on U.S. November: U.S. freezes funds of al-Barakaat for suspected links with al-Qaeda.

2002: In October, 21 warring factions and the TNG sign a cease-fire; peace talks begin in the Kenyan town of Eldoret.

2003: Cease-fire broken in Mogadishu as renewed fighting kills more than 50.

2004: After warring factions reach a peace deal, newest Transitional Federal Government (TFG) is inaugurated in Kenya and selects Abdullahi Yusuf Ahmed as president.

2006: Puntland adopts Sharia law. TFG parliament meets for the first time in Baidoa. After battles that kill hundreds, Islamic Court Union rules most of southern Somalia for six months, until Ethiopian and TFG troops take control of Mogadishu in December.

2007: Throughout the year, displaced Islamist groups stage attacks on federal and Ethiopian forces. U.N.-backed African Union peacekeepers arrive in Somalia.

2008: Moderate Islamist Sheikh Sharif Sheikh Ahmed becomes president; Islamist groups stage attacks hours after he arrives in Mogadishu.

2009: Omar Abdirashid Ali Sharmarke becomes prime minister. Three pirates are killed in a standoff with the U.S. Navy. Abdirahman Mohamud Farole elected president of Puntland. During a month-long fight with government forces, al-Shabaab attacks President Sharif's residence.

anjeero: flat bread, similar to a pancake.

aqal: a domed home, built of sticks and woven grasses and typically used by Somali nomads.

clan: a large group of people linked by male descent from a common ancestor (whose name is also the name of the clan).

dayr: Somalia's rainy season running from October to November.

dik-dik: a small antelope that lives in northern Somalia and along its rivers.

gross domestic product (GDP): the total value of all goods and services produced in a country in a one-year period.

gu: Somalia's rainy season running from April to June.

hadith: the body of traditions relating to the prophet Muhammad, which supplements the teachings of the Qur'an.

hagaa: Somalia's dry season lasting from July through September.

Haud: the geographic region extending across the width of Somalia from Hargeysa in the north to Gaalkacyo in the south, with lush vegetation during the rainy season.

hawala: a money transfer system used by Muslims worldwide.

henna: a plant-based dye used to decorate the hands and feet and color the hair.

International Monetary Fund: an agency affiliated with the United Nations that provides conditional loans, usually to developing countries.

jiilal: Somalia's dry season running from early January to late March.

lineage: the line of descendants, as traced from a common ancestor; in Somalia, the ancestor is male, and descent is traced through males.

macaawiis: a man's sarong or long wrap skirt.

monsoon: a seasonal wind of the Indian Ocean and southern Asia that frequently brings rains.

otka: dried camel meat that has been fried in butter and spices; it is used by nomads to provide nourishment during long journeys.

Pan-Somali: relating to or involving Pan-Somalism, the belief that present Somalia should be united with Somali-inhabited areas of Kenya, the Republic of Djibouti, and the Ogaden region of Ethiopia.

GLOSSARY

pastoral nomad: a member of a tribe that moves from place to place to find food and water, as well as pasture for its livestock.

plateau: a flat expanse of land at elevation.

Qur'an: Islam's holiest book; also spelled "Koran."

remittance: money that is sent to someone living far away.

Somali shilling: the currency of Somalia since national independence in 1960; divided into 100 Somali cents (centesimi).

soor: porridge, usually made of sorghum.

sorghum: a cereal grain native to Africa.

World Bank: informal name for a group of three affiliated financial institutions: the International Bank for Reconstruction and Development (IBRD), the International Development Association (IDA), and the International Finance Corporation (IFC); membership in the IMF is necessary to participate.

Ahmed, Ali Jimale, ed. *The Invention of Somalia*. Lawrenceville, N.J.: Red Sea Press, 1995.

Andrzejewski, B. W., and Sheila Andrzejewski. *Somali Poetry*. Bloomington: Indiana University Press, 1993.

Barnes, Virginia Lewe. *Aman: The Story of a Somali Girl*. New York: Pantheon Books, 1994.

Dirie, Waris, and Cathleen Miller. *Desert Flower: The Extraordinary Journey of a Desert Nomad*. New York: William Morrow and Co., 1998.

Frushone, Joel. *Welcome Home to Nothing: Refugees Repatriate to a Forgotten Somaliland*. Immigration and Refugee Services of America, 2001.

Ghalib, Jama. *The Cost of Dictatorship: The Somali Experience*. New York: Lilian Barber Press, 1995.

Henze, Paul B. *The Horn of Africa*. New York: MacMillan, 1991.

Hodd, Michael, ed. East Africa Handbook. Chicago: Passport Books, 1995.

Lewis, Ioan. *Understanding Somalia and Somaliland: Culture, History, Society*. New York: Columbia University Press, 2008.

Osman, Abdulahi A., and Issaka K. Souaré, eds. *Somalia at the Crossroads: Challenges and Perspectives in Reconstituting a Failed State*. London: Adonis & Abbey Publishers, Ltd., 2007.

Sahnoun, Mohamed. *Somalia: The Missed Opportunities*. Washington, D.C.: United States Institute Peace Press, 1994.

INTERNET RESOURCES

http://www.pbs.org/wgbh/pages/frontline/shows/ambush/

Ambush in Mogadishu: background information on the U.N. peacekeeping mission in Somalia, and the battle between U.S. troops and warlord Mohammad Farrah Aidid's forces; from the PBS program *Frontline*.

http://www.columbia.edu/cu/lweb/indiv/africa/cuvl/Somalia.html

Somalia and Somaliland: Links to resources from the African Studies Department of Columbia University.

http://www.somalianews.com/

Somalia News: latest information on Somalia from various news sources; includes links to websites sponsored by Western and African media.

http://www.africa.upenn.edu/Country_Specific/Somalia.html

The Somalia Page, from the African Studies Department at the University of Pennsylvania, contains links to current resources on Somalia.

Numbers in **bold italic** refer to captions.

INDEX

INDEX/PICTURE CREDITS

The **FOREIGN POLICY RESEARCH INSTITUTE (FPRI)** served as editorial consultants for the MAJOR MUSLIM NATIONS series. FPRI is one of the nation's oldest "think tanks." The Institute's Middle East Program focuses on Gulf security, monitors the Arab-Israeli peace process, and sponsors an annual conference for teachers on the Middle East, plus periodic briefings on key developments in the region.

Among the FPRI's trustees is a former Secretary of State and a former Secretary of the Navy (and among the FPRI's former trustees and interns, two current Undersecretaries of Defense), not to mention two university presidents emeritus, a foundation president, and several active or retired corporate CEOs.

The scholars of FPRI include a former aide to three U.S. Secretaries of State, a Pulitzer Prize–winning historian, a former president of Swarthmore College and a Bancroft Prize–winning historian, and two former staff members of the National Security Council. And the FPRI counts among its extended network of scholars—especially its Inter-University Study Groups—representatives of diverse disciplines, including political science, history, economics, law, management, religion, sociology, and psychology.

DR. HARVEY SICHERMAN is president and director of the Foreign Policy Research Institute in Philadelphia, Pennsylvania. He has extensive experience in writing, research, and analysis of U.S. foreign and national security policy, both in government and out. He served as Special Assistant to Secretary of State Alexander M. Haig Jr. and as a member of the Policy Planning Staff of Secretary of State James A. Baker III. Dr. Sicherman was also a consultant to Secretary of the Navy John F. Lehman Jr. (1982–1987) and Secretary of State George Shultz (1988).

A graduate of the University of Scranton (B.S., History, 1966), Dr. Sicherman earned his Ph.D. at the University of Pennsylvania (Political Science, 1971), where he received a Salvatori Fellowship. He is author or editor of numerous books and articles, including *America the Vulnerable: Our Military Problems and How to Fix Them* (FPRI, 2002) and *Palestinian Autonomy, Self-Government and Peace* (Westview Press, 1993). He edits *Peacefacts*, an FPRI bulletin that monitors the Arab-Israeli peace process.

LEEANNE GELLETLY is a freelance writer and editor living outside Philadelphia, Pennsylvania. She has written biographies of Harriet Beecher Stowe and Mae Jemison, and geography books on South American countries.